BANJALUKA

PUBLISHER:
Novinsko preduzeće GLAS, Banjaluka 1970.

Editor-in-chief
MILJKO ŠINDIĆ

Art and Layout Editor
ENVER ŠTALJO

The region of Bosanska Krajina, with Banjaluka as its natural, political and cultural centre, has always been a markedly militant part of Bosnia, vitally linked with the liberal movements in the other parts of Yugoslavia. Its border-line position and revolutionary past have conditioned, to a great extent, the character and the mentality of its people, hardened through centuries of struggle and determined not to give in to violence and injustice, and to overcome the worst hardships. United by their common destiny, they have drawn through such struggles nameless strength from their own being, and went beyond human limits in the shaping of their own history and survival on native soil. In this respect, Banjaluka and the Bosanska Krajina are an outstanding example of human relationships, both in joy and creation and in suffering and hardship.

Banjaluka, the town spreading along the banks of the clear Vrbas, with its picturesque and fertile environs, orchards and flower gardens, odorous rows of chestnuts and linden trees, with its vast plain stretching from the Gornji Šeher all the way to the Sava, inspired already in old times writers of travels, poets and builders, but it also attracted numerous aliens and invaders. However, whenever they came, and no matter how long they remained, they never succeeded in degenerating the town. Even in the darkest times of its history, Banjaluka always remained unwavering and true to its native soil. That is why the people of Krajina have always considered the town their own, and have always been fatefully united with it. Its ancient monuments still remind of the stormy past: the large Kastel fortress, situated in the middle of the town, the stone walls of which are washed by the Vrbas, the architecturally extremely harmonious mosques Ferhadija and Arnaudija with their slender minarets, built in the 16th century during Turkish rule over Bosnia, the monasteries and churches Gomionica, Petrićevac and Trapisti, and — in the picturesque Gornji Šeher — the ancient Roman and Turkish baths.

Banjaluka is known as a town which fosters and promotes freedom and brotherhood; it is also a town of youth and song. Banjaluka is a town of human solidarity, and of resistance which stops at nothing when freedom and human dignity are involved. This spirit of Banjaluka and of the Bosanska Krajina has been expressed powerfully by the numerous brave and eminent people in its past, perservering fighters for the liberation of our people from foreign oppression, who fought for land reforms in Bosnia and Herzegovina, were precursors of socialist ideas and introduced Bosnian man into modern literature (Vaso Pelagić, Petar Kočić, Ivan Franjo Jukić, Gavrilo Princip, Hasan Kikić), and by the countless generations of revolutionaries from the pre-war workers' movement and from the People's Liberation War and revolution. Their work still inspires the people of this town in their endeavours to create and build a better and juster society. Through its dynamic social, cultural and economic growth, Banjaluka keeps pace with our time, strengthening and promoting those social forces that give its overall development a deeply democratic and humane socialist character.

A monument to the heroism, hardships and victories of the Krajina in the revolution rises proudly on the hill of Šehitluci, on the slopes of the mountain Starčevica north of Banjaluka, where a meeting was held — in June of 1941 — on the preparations and beginning of the People's War of Liberation in the Bosanska Krajina. This monument speaks to the young generations about the 22 brigades of fighters from the Krajina and from Banjaluka who led — for full four years — a bitter struggle against the invaders and the native traitors, both in the Bosanska Krajina and all over the country, and spread the glory of the Krajina throughout Yugoslavia. It speak about the epics of the Kozara, about the courage of the people from Grmeč, Drvar, Petrovac. Janjane, Glamoč, Zmijanje, about the victories won at Prijedor, Bihać, Jajce, Banjaluka, Kotor-Varoš, Velika Kladuša, Bosanska Krupa and other Krajina towns (according to the official data of the Republican Committee of the Veterans' Association, during the People's Liberation War the Bosanska Krajina, together with Banjaluka, gave 64,311 fighters and 123 people's heroes. More than 80,000 people lost their lives in the war — 19,822 partisans, 10,377 in concentration camps, and more than 50,000 in the massacres and prisons all over the region. The heroes and the victims hewn into the reliefs of the monument speak of the high price of freedom, of the might of united people. The images of the monument express the power and the greatness of the revolution, the heroism and the self-sacrifice of our people, and especially that of youth. Its symbols, the invader vanquished by the fighting people, are only a continuation of the resistance spirit of this town and region since ancient times, from the struggle against Turkish tyranny and brutal Austrian oppression to the victory of the revolution.

It was in the Krajina that the vital decision was made concerning the further development and organization of the people's liberation army into modern armed forces, organized in major military units — divisions and corps. On the free soil of the Bosanska Krajina a fraternal community was created — the future Federal Republic of Bosnia and Herzegovina — as an expression of the historic aspirations of the Serbs, Croats and Moslems, and as the result of their victories in the People's Liberation War and revolution. At the same time, the community of free and equal peoples — Democratic Federal Yugoslavia — was founded in the Krajina, through the common will of all Yugoslav peoples and nationalities.

If one bears in mind the entire hard and revolutionary past, the role, the share and the victims of Bosanska Krajina and Banjaluka during the People's Liberation War and the revolution, one may easily understand the reason why the people of this region again demonstrated all the virtues of their past and more recent revolutionary history in the October of 1969, when the town and its environs suffered the greatest tragedy in their history, when the terrifying elements destroyed an enormous number of homes, hospitals, schools, cultural institutions, monuments and other values created through centuries, razed to the ground or severely damaged a great number of modern industrial and other plants, unbalancing and bringing to a standstill the entire economy of the region built by thousands of diligent human hands over the two and a half decades after the Liberation. That was another impulse which stirred the entire country, and many foreign friends, to noble solidarity with Banjaluka and the Bosanska Krajina, and to the urgent provision of assistance.

In the immediate action taken to alleviate the consequences of the disastrous earthquake, and in the common endeavours to reconstruct the Bosanska Krajina permanently, new and precious experience was acquired, and the vitality, knowledge, readiness and determination of all the factors of the self--governing socialist society was checked. All the self-government bodies — the social and political ones in the commune, local communities, enterprises, hospitals, schools and other institutions, functioned efficiently from the very beginning, marking the outstanding self-organizing spirit of citizens, political activists, experts and services. The health service deserves special mention, although its facilities were severely affected. Since it involved mostly people who were ill and unable to move, this activity required the utmost vigilance and self-organization. Maximum collective discipline was evidenced in such exceptional circumstances. All the warnings, instructions and recommendations of the Town Council and of the Civil Defense Staff were readily accepted and implemented. The citizens left their homes and spent the cold night in the open, in cars, buses, garages etc. Teaching in schools was stopped; ill and old people and children were moved out of damaged buildings.

Such an activity of the self-government and social bodies was made possible by the self-sacrificing and devoted work of the numerous members and organizations of the League of Communists, the Socialist Alliance, the Youth Organization, the Veterans' Association, etc. During those days, the efforts of these organizations were turned to the solution of the town's most urgent problems, and their members showed the highest degree of socialist and self-government consciousness, thereby enriching their experience and knowledge.

The Yugoslav People's Army — from the privates to the highest commanding staff — joined such an overall human activity and mobility in a very successful and organized way. It provided major assistance to the people and organizations in the town and surrounding settlements. While buildings were still crumbling down, army units had already begun to clear the ruins, to rescue and provide first aid to injured citizens. Together with the local communities, the army set up the first tent settlements for the homeless population, handed out the first warm meals, helped in supplying drinking water, took part in health actions through its specialized teams, protected the property in the damaged shops and warehouses, provided for the necessary telephone lines. All these activities, omnipresent in the town and its surroundings, created in these extraordinary circumstances a feeling of self-confidence and calm. Altogether, they made up an imposing picture of a unique joint action of the army and the people, and showed clearly how a practical coordinated action between the army and the municipal self-government bodies should look like. This may serve as a precious experience for similar situations involving the defense of the country.

Thanks to all these actions, the next earthquake on the following day — although much more powerful, and although it now destroyed completely the formerly damaged flats, schools and plants — caused no casualties. That was no chance. The absence of casualties is a clear proof of the organizing and functioning ability of a self-governing social system in exceptional circumstances. Once again this proved that man is the fundamental value, and the rescue and protection of human lives is the most essential thing of all. This is the best reflection of the humane socialist relations in our society.

In spite of the common effort, Banjaluka and the Bosanska Krajina are having a hard time. People are living in sheds, camping trailers, waggons, garages and huts. Children are born here, the first letters learnt, and the first knowledge acquired. In demolished Banjaluka and other towns and villages, whose chief vital veins have been broken, people work and create faced with huge difficulties; but, at the same time, the spirit of the town and of the Krajina keeps living and defying every hardship. New heroes, heroes of work, are being born out of this struggle with the numerous trials, out of the efforts to heal the wounds inflicted by the earthquake; these are the builders of the new Banjaluka and the new Krajina, the carriers of the firm faith that this land will again develop and live a full life.

In the present-day world of an ever more developing engineering civilization, and an ever deeper gap between the rich and the poor, one of the most dramatic contradictions is human alienation and indifference. And yet, man's alienation in the modern world, the basic roots of which may be sought in the obsolete social relations in which he lives and works, is opposed by the prospect offered by the democratic and progressive forces which fight for more humane and juster relationships among people, for the full recognition of those that create truly human values, for a more rational and juster distribution of the created wealth. In this context, the solidarity aroused in our country and in the world by the earthquake in the Bosanska Krajina, which may also be witnessed in similar instances all over the world, restores faith into man whose entire spiritual development is based on the struggle for the humanization of human relationships.

The hand of solidarity was extended to the Bosanska Krajina not only by our people, but also by many other countries. Ill-fortune brings people together, especially when the wounds are still fresh. Wounds of this kind take a long time to heal, and require a lot of courage and self-denial; no first assistance is sufficient, and years will pass before normal life begins: for the elements have destroyed, in a brief moment, the patient human work of centuries.

The idea of the Glas Newspaper-Publishing Enterprise to edit a photo-monograph on the past and present of Banjaluka and Bosanska Krajina, and to present — through picture and word — the reality and true meaning of its people's strife, is a part of the great and noble efforts made to preserve and reconstruct the Banjaluka and the Bosanska Krajina as we used to know it, to rebuild everything — spiritual and material — that had been created to the moment of disaster and that was damaged and destroyed by the earthquake. This publication is concurrently the expression of the need to acknowledge humane and noble aims — which, where persevering, will vanquish nature's most destructive elements.

Osman Karabegović

Banjaluka, the largest town of northwestern Bosnia, with seventy-five thousand inhabitants, and the second largest town in the Socialist Republic Bosnia and Herzegovina, lies in the southern part of the Banjaluka Plain, on both banks of the river Vrbas which pushes, after Jajce, through picturesque canyons, then crosses the area of tertiary hills and descends, downstream of Banjaluka, into the vast plains of the Posavina. The oldest settlement in the town, Gornji Šeher, is situated below the cliffs of the Vrbas canyon, between the hill Šehitluci and the Jajačke Stijene cliffs.

Archaeological discoveries (findings from the bronze age in Kazavida near Bosanska Gradiška, in Orašje on the Sava, and Griča near Mrkonjić-Grad) show that the area round Banjaluka, in the basin of the Vrbas and Vrbanja rivers, was inhabited by the great Illyrian tribe — the Moesi — in pre-Roman times.

For almost two hundred years Illyrian tribes resisted Roman conquest. Only in 9 A. D. were they finally conquered by the Roman general Germanicus.

In Roman times Banjaluka was crossed by the road from Salona to Servitium (present-day Bosanska Gradiška), which continued farther to Sisak. Military fortifications — Castra — were set up in the town and in its environments, on the spot of the present-day Kastel: Ad Ladios (near Trn), and Ad Fines (near Laktaši). Archaeological findings disclosed the existence of another Roman settlement in the Gornji Šeher area. In the 6th and 7th century this region was settled by the Slavs. Since the Roman garrisons retreated, and traffic on the Salona — Sisak road was interrupted, the former Roman settlements began to decline.

Few historical sources speak of the life and importance of Banjaluka during the mediaeval Bosnian state. It is known, however, that it was under the rule of the Hrvatinić Dukes, as part of a region called Donji Kraji (Lower Lands).

The first record of the town's present-day name is found in a deed of the Hungaro-Croatian king Wladislaw II which mentions Juraj Mikulašić as the castellan of Banjaluka. At the time the castle was in the Gornji Šeher area, while the town — with the Franciscan monastery — spread below.

Along with this fortified town, the following mediaeval towns existed in the environs of Banjaluka: Vrbaški Grad (since the 12th century), Zvečaj, Krupa, Zemljanik, Bočac, Kotor and Berbir. Vrbaški Grad (which, most proably, stood on the spot of present-day Kastel) was an important fortification, which is confirmed by the letter of Hrvoje Vukčić to Queen Barbara, wife of

DUBICA 1239 g.

Knežica

...dičevo ...0 g. ?

...jgrad

Župa Dubica XIII v.

Vojska 1249 g.

Sv. Grgur

Podgraci 1334 g.

Kobaš XII v.

Turjak 1334 g. Sv. Mihajlo

Sv. Martin Kozara 1334 g.

Ivanjska 1334 g.

Župa Vrbas 1244 g.

Sv. Nik...

Dragi-družac Podgradie 1446 g.

Sri...

Sv. Marko Sv. Martin Japra XIV v.

BLAGAJSKI

Župa Sana XIII v.

Sana

Vrbaški grad (Banja Luka) 1244 g.

Vrbanja 1322 g.

Župa G... XIII v.

Tukleka Oko 1331 g.

Župa Ukrin...

Kola 1287 g.

ZVEČAJ 1404 g. Dvorac vojvode Hrvoja Vukčića

Župa Zemljanik XIII v.

Liplje 1273 g.

SANICA

Peći

Mrin XIV v.

Kotor 1322 g.

Ribić XIV v.

Župa Mrin

(Krupa) Greben 1192 g.

ZEMLJANIK 1287 g.

Pribinovci 1446 g.

Klevci

Lušci 1306 g.

KLJUČ 1322 g.

Župa Vrbanja 1322 g.

Župa Banice XIII v.

BANICE 1244 g.

Bočac 1446 i 1494 g.

Podstinje 1323 g.

Župa Luka XII v.

Vlatkovići

Mile 1322 g.

Komotin XV v.

Jezero Sv. Grgur 1447 g.

Sv. Katarina Sv. Luka Sv. Marija

JAJCE XV v.

Guča gora 1425 g.

Sokograd 1363 g.

Župa Pliva XV v.

Vinac 1453 g.

O

Tra... 1463...

VUKČIĆ-HRVATINIĆI

Vrbas

Turići ? XV v.

B

Župa...

Prusac (Biograd)

Žu...

King Sigmund, in which he pledged Vrbaški Grad and Kozara to the king as token of his fidelity.

In 1528 the Turks conquered the Province of Jajce and Banjaluka together with the other fortifications.

With the Turks' arrival Banjaluka began to spread rapidly, to become the largest urban settlement in northwestern Bosnia. In 1533 the seat of the Bosnian Sanjak-Bey was transferred from Sarajevo to Bosnia, and Banjaluka became the political centre of Bosnia. The Sanjak-Bey Sofi Mohammed-Pasha built, in the Gornji Šeher, a bridge across the Vrbas near the Imperial Mosque, a public bath, a large hostelry and caravanserai, four mills and 59 shops. According to old writings, crafts needed by the army and citizens were developed in the town: tanners, sabre-makers, boot-makers, boot-leg-makers and millers. Parallelly with the spreading of the town and growth of its population, other crafts appeared: blacksmiths, tailors, butchers, bakers, halvah-makers, soap--makers... At the time the Gornji Šeher consisted of nine districts, five on the right and four on the left bank of the Vrbas.

Bosnia became a pashalik (beylerbeylic) in 1580, and Banjaluka became an administrative seat of a higher order. The first beylerbey, Ferhad-Pasha Sokolović, started building the Donji (Lower) Šeher between the Vrbas and Crkvena. Up to 1587 Ferhad-Pasha had 216 public buildings built, the most important having been the Ferhadija Mosque, the elementary school, the mausoleum, a fountain and public bath with a separate waterworks, the watch--tower, a caravanserai, etc. In the same period (1595) the Arnaudija Mosque was built, "this wonderful palace and magnificent work of art", intended for "a pleasant meeting place of good people", according to the verses hewn into the stone slab above the entrance.

The picturesqueness of Banjaluka was further enhanced by the lush greenery and opulence of its gardens and orchards. The known Turkish travelogue writer Evlija Čelebija, who passed through Banjaluka in 1660 and 1664, left us a record of this: "Out of the many fruits, cherries are so sweet, succulent and tasty as to have no equal in European Turkey, Arabia or Persia. The area is also known by its quinces and apples... Among drinks, famous are goat's milk, whey, mead, sour cherry juice, mustard extract, wormwood and "nana" extracts. Altogether about five thousand vineyards and orchards pay the vineyard tax."

Because of its strategic importance, during the 16th and 17th century Banjaluka was further developed, and became a major economic centre, with a well-developed communal structure, crafts activities and trade. In the early

17th century the town on the Vrbas got its first café, much before many other large European towns. With its 45 streets, Banjaluka had more than 400 shops, 4,000 houses and about 20,000 inhabitants of Moslem, Catholic and Orthodox faith. The local traders developed very lively traffic connections with Sarajevo, Split, Venice, Skopje, Salonika and Istanbul. The produce sold were cattle and honey, clothing and leather products, gold and silver jewels.

In 1639 the seat of the Bosnian pashalik was again transferred to Sarajevo, which brought the further growth of the town to a relative standstill. After 1688 the town was raided, from time to time, by Austrian troops. In 1737 a great and important battle was fought below the walls of the Kastel, in which the Austrian general Hildenburghausen suffered defeat. He retreated, leaving six thousand dead soldiers and a ravaged town. On several occasions the town was also burnt to the ground by disastrous fires. Fires caused major damage in the town in 1688, 1724, 1869 and 1878. The third major disaster for the inhabitants of Banjaluka was plague. It raged in 1690, 1732, and from 1813 to 1818. The 1732 epidemics was particularly severe and seven thousand people died.

The time of Banjaluka's ascent under Turkish rule soon passed. The "lean years" — the time of decline and suffering — started in the late 17th century and lasted up to the second half of the 19th century. Folk art: songs, dances, embroidery and engraving, have always been the deepest expression of people's life, their apprehensions, forebodings and feelings. This ancient spirit has been preserved to the present day. C o u n t r y s o n g s from the environs of Banjaluka, poor in type but rich in intonation and slight rhythm changes, full of inner splendour and beauty, "dark, flashy and triumphal" at the same time, leave the "impression of primeval swelling". In the towns the s e v d a-
l i n k a (Bosnian love song) flourished to the accompaniment of the "šargija" (kind of stringed instrument). The m u t e d a n c e of the Krajina, which starts with the song of the young men and girl who »seem to imitate the wind or the storm", and the ornament in e m b r o i d e r y and e n g r a v i n g, are simple in their restraint, but rich and fanciful in the deep meaning of their forms.

Until the 17th century there are no reliable data on the work of schools in Banjaluka. The elementary literacy could be acquired only in mon-asteries, in the religious elementary schools of the Moslems, or from rare individuals — transcribers. In 1832 the Serbian religious school for boys was established, followed — in 1864 — by the girls' school. In the latter year the Croatian religious school also started working and — in 1872 — the school run by the nuns. In 1873 the Banjaluka sanjak (province) had 75 elementary schools for boys and girls. In 1866 the Serbian Orthodox seminary — which trained the teachers for the province — was instituted in Banjaluka.

An important personality in the Banjaluka of the time was Ivan Franjo Jukić Banjalučanin (1818—1857), the "unhappy and diligent Illyrian from Bosnia", as they called him. Ethnographer, writer of travels, storyteller and historian, Jukić described folk customs, collected folk songs and stories, promoted the B o s n i a n F r i e n d, the first literary journal in Bosnia (1850), took active part in the establishment of schools and printing works, wrote stories and textbooks. Jukić drew the attention of Bosnian people to their links with other Yugoslav lands and peoples. He was a torch-bearer and educator — both by his devotion to his tasks and by his actual work.

Vaso Pelagić appeared towards the end of Turkish rule. His endeavours bore the imprint of the difficulties affecting educational work of the time. As the originator and headmaster of the Seminary, he tried to develop it into a "small university", the spiritual focus of the struggle against ignorance and tyranny. Accused that his students were more like soldiers than students, and that they incited people to revolt against authority, Pelagić was finally tried and sentenced, while his school was closed down. His journalistic work, in which he presented himself as the first Bosnian socialist, would follow only later on — although not in Banjaluka but outside Bosnia — in Serbia.

An interesting picture of the Banjaluka of the time was drawn by the known "Illyrian" Ivan Kukuljević Sakcinski, who visited the town in 1857: "All the Banjaluka houses have one floor. In the middle of the streets mud is knee-high; only the edges, where people walk, are paved with small stones, but people say the paving dates back to Kulin Ban, which would make it more than 700 years old ... Numerous shops, made — according to Eastern custom — of boards, huddle together in the market. One already sees a lot of trifles from Vienna and Trieste, which will not make Bosnia too happy."

Twenty years later the French journalist Charles Yriarte painted a more serene picture of Banjaluka in his book on Bosnia and Herzegovina: "The street is very wide, bordered by trees, and it passes next to lush gardens with various plants among which one notices — from time to time — the grey stones of Turkish tombstones ... The Turkish town starts behind the gardens and it is wider and more picturesque than the Serbian district; the bazaar is very wide, with a large mosque in the middle."

In 1869 the first telephone line connected Banjaluka with Sarajevo, Bihać and Bosanska Gradiška. In the same years the trappist arrived to Banjaluka. They built a large mill, a brewery, brickworks, weaving mill, sawmill and — after the Austrians occuried Banjaluka — the hydroelectric power station in Delibašino Selo. In January, 1873, the first standard gauge railway in Bosnia — from Banjaluka to Dobrljin (104 kilometres) — was completed and opened for traffic.

The Bosnian-Herzegovinian Uprising of 1875 caused significant changes in Bosnia and Herzegovina, drawing the attention of the European political public to these lands. The great powers, under the pretext of enforcing order in Bosnia and Herzegovina, decided — at the Berlin Congress in 1878 — that Austria should occupy these regions. Austrian troops entered Banjaluka on July 31, 1878. A fortnight later the Krajina Moslems attacked Banjaluka with the intention of liberating the town, but their attempt failed. The Austrians burned down the market, and killed the prisoners or exiled them. In his short story U n d e r A r m s, the Croatian writer Eugen Kumičić has left us a very impressive picture of Banjaluka during those dramatic events: "We were all aghast when we arrived near the market, to the nice mosque which rises next to the very gates of the fort. Stinking and black smoke blew in the gloomy air and round the sleek minarets, sparks flew everywhere; remains left by fire are found everywhere and many houses still burn, blames burst from shops, everything is crumbling down, breaking, shattering . . ."

Through the investment of capital into the economy of Bosnia and Herzegovina, the Austrohungarian monarchy started exploiting its natural wealth and preparing for further expansion. Private capital was granted major privileges. Foreigners began to arrive to Banjaluka, especially from Austria, Hungary and Czechoslovakia. Among the newcomers there were also different professionals. They exercised considerable influence on the development of crafts and catering. In order to attain their objectives, the new masters of Bosnia and Herzegovina began to build railways and roads, open up mines, industrial plants, and introduced their own administration. The penetration of foreign capital also strengthened local bourgeoisie. The development of industry created the working class which, although in its infancy, soon began to organize its ranks in the struggle for its rights. As early as in 1904 the first strike was organized by the garment-workers. In 1906 the workers of Banjaluka took part in the general strike of the workers of Bosnia and Herzegovina.

In 1880 the Austrian authorities opened the first state school. Five years later the Commercial School enrolled its first students. The Banjaluka High School, which would play an very important role in the cultural and political life of Banjaluka and of the Bosanska Krajina, was instituted in 1895.

The Higher Girls' School was opened in 1898. Banjaluka got its first printing shop in 1886, and two more soon afterwards.

During Turkish rule settlements were built along the banks of the Vrbas. The Austrohungarian authorities built new settlements and streets farther away from the river, and the town began to spread north of the Ferhad-Pasha Mosque. The tradition of planting tree avenues was continued. Thus, Banjaluka retained the character of a "garden town". In 1908 the single-storey building of the hospital was erected, and the pavilion for infectious diseases, which replaced the "hastehana" from the Turkish period.

In the beginning of the twentieth century the Banjaluka area yielded one of Bosnia's outstanding political tribunes, and one of the best storytellers in the literature of Yugoslav peoples — Petar Kočić (1877—1916), whose works immortalized this world in its vital essence. Kočić's literary work presents the Krajina snowstorms and hardships, evokes the dreams and discourses of this world from the m o u n t a i n and b e l o w t h e m o u n t a i n, grasps the wondrous link between the spiritual and the acrid, the sad and the witty, in the rugged mood of the Krajina man, weaves the threads of reality, laughter and myth which twist throughout the texture of his living. By their traits of elementary power and tempestuous vital unrestraint, by the melancholic thread and dramatic swing of m i s t and l i g h t, Kočić's stories bear the imprint of the Krajina spirit and life in their most authentic form.

Kočić started and edited the newspapers O t a d ž b i n a (Homeland) (1907) and R a z v i t a k (Development) (1910). Round Kočić there rallied, at the time, a group of cultural, literary and political workers. Some of the most outstanding Yugoslav writers and ethnographers of the time also wrote in those newspapers and, thus, provided their contribution to their cultural action. Owing to their militant political attitudes, Kočić and the Otadžbina group were tried and sentenced in the days of the annexation crsis.

The Bosnian Krajina entered World War One with its heavy burden of national and social contrasts. From November 3, 1915, to March 16, 1916, a deliberately construed high treason trial was held in Banjaluka against 156 patriots — intellectuals, tradesmen, farmers and students. European and world press followed the trial. 16 Serbs were sentenced to death, and 81 to hard labour. The sentences provoked the indignant protests of the liberal public, and the alien authorities had to pardon all those sentenced to death.

After the fall of the Austrohungarian Monarchy, the Kingdom of the Serbs, Croats and Slovenes was created by the Treaty of Versailles in 1918. In the new, united state, our peoples expected to see the realization of the hopes for which they had, for centuries, aspired and fought; they looked forward to national equality and freedom. But, one kind of national oppression was replaced by another, and the social exploitation of the workers by the national burgeoisie continued in all its intensity. Unemployment set in. Farmers, which made up 70 percent of the population, were indebted and without any rights, burdened by taxes and the economic crisis.

In 1922 Banjaluka became the seat of the Prefect of the Vrbas region. Several schools were established during the time, e. g. the Lower Agricultural School (1923), the Training-School and the Communal Coeducational School (1925). They were later on followed by the Higher School of Commerce, Engineering School, Agricultural-Housekeeping School, and Trade School. Banjaluka became the school centre of the Krajina, and the centre of educational, cultural and political activities.

After Banjaluka became the centre of the Vrbas Province, i. e. of northwestern Bosnia (1929), new buildings were erected: the Prefect's Palace and the provincial administration building, the Hypothecary Bank, a representative orthodox church, the modern building of the Surgery Ward of the hospital, the Institute of Hygiene, the Health Centre, and numerous blocks of flats for the provincial administration employees.

The National Theatre of Banjaluka, which is still one of the most important cultural institutions in this area, gave its first performance in 1930. In the same year the Ethnographic Museum opened its gates to the public. Several attempts were made to revive and continue Kočić's literary tradition. Culture-literary reviews were published: Književna Krajina (The Literary Krajina, 1931—1932) and Razvitak (Development, 1935—1941).

Banjaluka's most important personality in the field of ideological and spiritual creativity between the two wars was the revolutionary and Marxist journalist Veselin Masleša (born in Banjaluka in 1906, died as one of the councillors of the AVNOJ on the Sutjeska in 1943). Masleša's activities among the progressive working and school youth of Banjaluka provided vital new impulses to the ideological and spiritual climate of the cultural reality of the Krajina. In his journalistic work, in his works on the Mlada (Young) Bosna movement, the Bosnian uprising, Pelagić and Kočić, Masleša threw light — from the standpoint of historic materialism — upon the historical reality of Bosnian life and its phenomena in the recent past.

Sanski Most, ceramics — 4th century B. C.

Vučedol Culture vessel found in the ruins of the
Zecovi Castle near Prijedor — Eneolithic

Hearth from Donja Dolina, 7th — 5th century B. C.

Boat from Donja Dolina, 10th — 8th century B. C.

Sanski Most, Greek ceramics — 3rd century B. C.

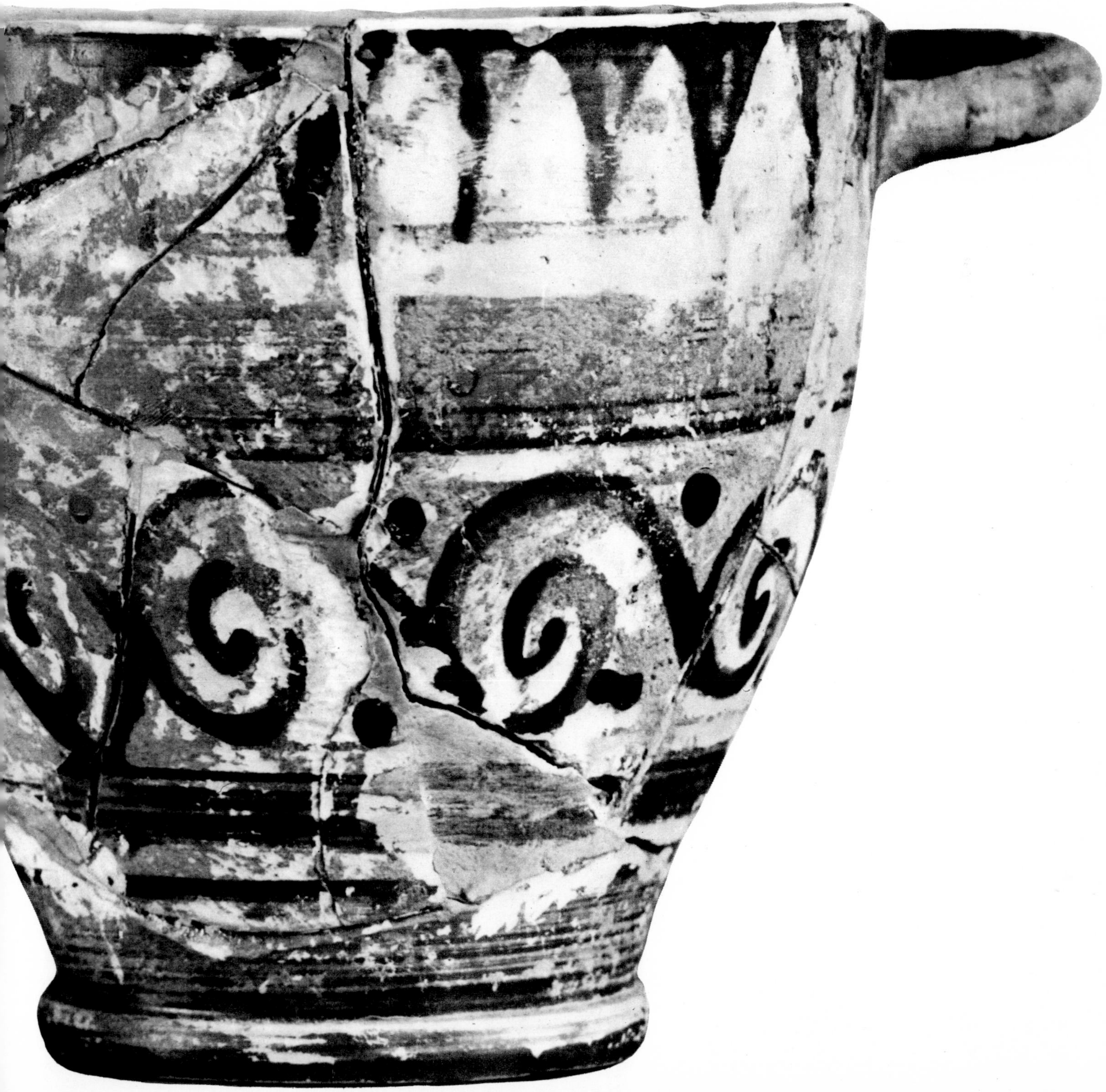

Belt buckle from Radosavska near Banjaluka, bronze, 8th century B. C.

Illyrian goddess from the Glamoč Valley

Vučedol Culture vessel from the Hrustovac Cave — Eneolithic

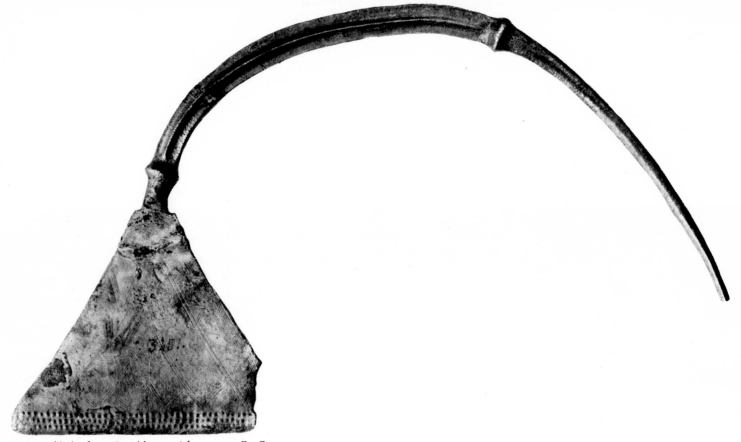

Bronze fibula from Ivanjska — 8th century B. C.

Vučedol Culture vessel — Eneolithic

Roman fountain in Banjaluka

Earthenware vessel from Donja Dolina — 4th century B. C.

Syrian deity Dolychen,
Japra — 3rd century

Medusa's head, Šipovo
— 3rd century

Relief of a horseman,
Divičani near Jajce —
3rd century

Ruins of a mausoleum,
Šipovo — 4th century

Relief of the god Mithras
Taurochton, Jajce — 4th
century

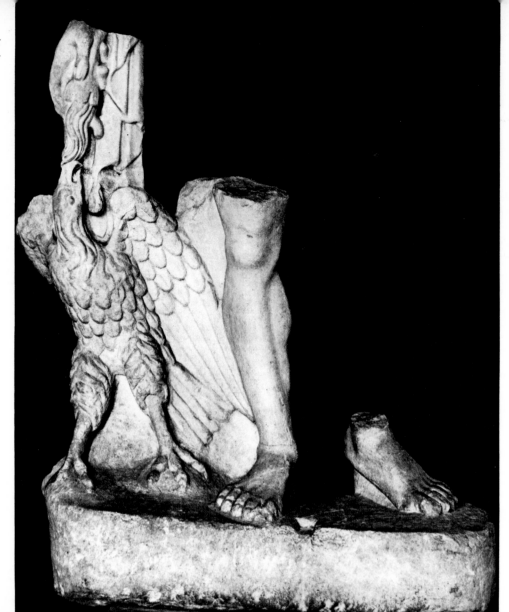

Fragment of statue of Jupiter with the eagle, Mala Ruiška — 3rd century

Roman sarcophagus, Banjaluka

Fragment of Capitoline Triad relief showing Jupiter and Minerva, Šipovo — 3rd century

Altar
dedicated to Jupiter
and to the genius loci,
Banjaluka — 3rd
century

Roman therms, Banjaluka

Roman fountain, Banjaluka

Altar dedicated to the goddess Earth
— 3rd century

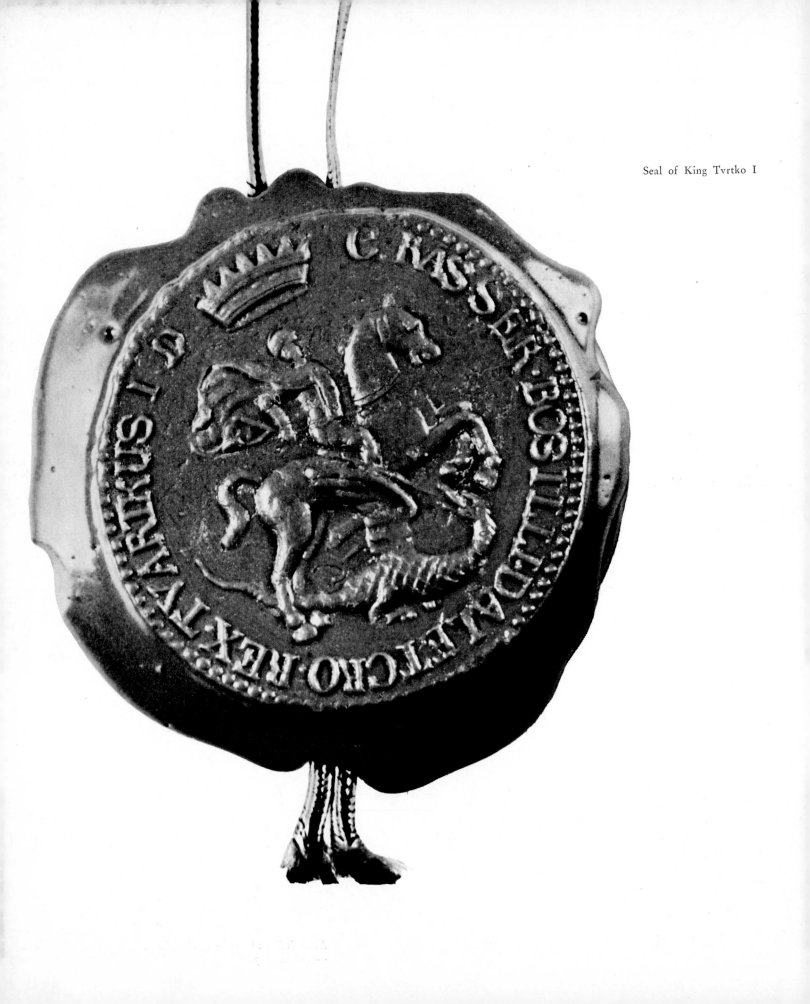

Seal of King Tvrtko I

Bogumil tombstone, Krupa on the Vrbas

Glagolitic inscription on stone, environs of Banjaluka, 15th century

Bogumil tombstone, Baljvine necropolis

Decoration motifs on
Bogumil tombstones,
Krupa on the Vrbas.

Mediaeval tower, Krupa
on the Vrbas — 12th
century

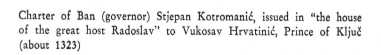

Charter of Ban (governor) Stjepan Kotromanić, issued in "the house of the great host Radoslav" to Vukosav Hrvatinić, Prince of Ključ (about 1323)

Coat-of-arms of
Hrvoje Vukčić, Jajce
— 15th century

St Luke's belfry:
In the mid-fifteenth century from the
Dalmatian shores the Romanesque
escaped in a basket —
it forgot the building
perfection bearing the Bosnian name.
Both the belfry and the minaret were
the index of the old town of Jajce.

Bogumil tombstone: the stone on the head curses birth, stone in the head
— dead spite, neither hungry nor miserable.

Fig. 39.

15*

Letters and miniatures from Hrvoje's Missal, written between 1403 and 1415, in the angular Glagolitic script, by the scholar Butko and dedicated to Hrvoje Vukčić Hrvatinić, Grand Duke of Bosnia and Duke of Split.

The Greben burg, 1192

Slab with Glagolitic inscription, Banjaluka — 15th century

It sleeps without our heads
bought for a hatful of copper coins
for a jugful of blood.
Painful to the steep hill,
and called Bočac.

KASTEL

Roman fort (third century?), next to Castra, Banjaluka's
forerunner — Bosanski Vrbaški Grad (1244), burned and
abandoned by its commander Andrija Radatović after the
conquest of Jajce by the Turks in 1527. — The Turkish fortress,
built by Ferhad-pasha Sokolović round 1587.

CASTLE

Ever more scowling for the evil age
For the forgotten gunpowder and hooves
A century caved on every stone
And an ancient spring on the towers
Writing the ballad of Safikada

The heavy gates
Have no more guards
Or sheiks
Or daggers
Or soldiers on the battlements
To grab from the scales
The thick cherries of Evlija Čelebija

Only the big gun
At the bottom of the Vrbas
Is enraptured by the green water

Antonije ĆOSIĆ

THE TREASURE OF ZVEČAJ

Quiet

the grandfather's hand lives in you
and shakes you
as a rattle
The shadow of the tower is larger than the sun
one wall only stops the wind
nobody drinks water from the dry fountain

midday peers behind the gray embrasures
the sun has risen as a helmet on a skull
a playing boy is really a god

from whence the gray fatigue of the tired stone
why does everything in death remind of life

The helmet of a long dead warrior along the river
the sun's club on the gray skull
nobody descends and nobody is aloft

who has thrown a stone in the air, like a black bird
the stone fell on the flesh of the tortuous river's sabre
the bent stone fell and burst into leaf
I threaten you with my hands and maces
stone wall: speak up or fall on me

Irfan HOROZOVIĆ

Zvečaj, the castle of Duke Hrvoje Vukčić (1404)

Moslem tombstones

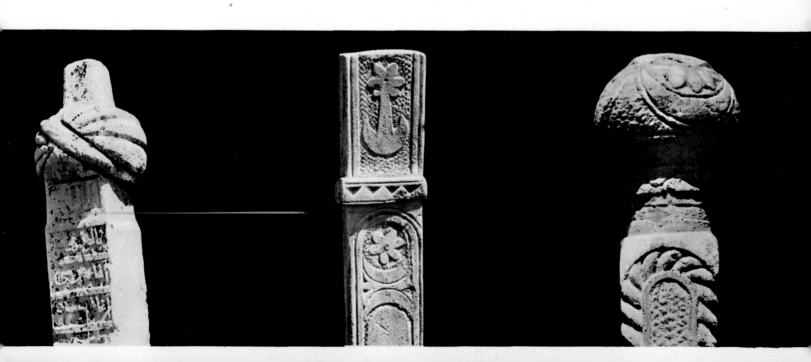

And from the vaults of the white building and from the swanlike neck
stiffened by desire with stars
there falls down the infinite dust
ot the crumbling minaret

The Gazanferija Mosque

Old Banjaluka gates

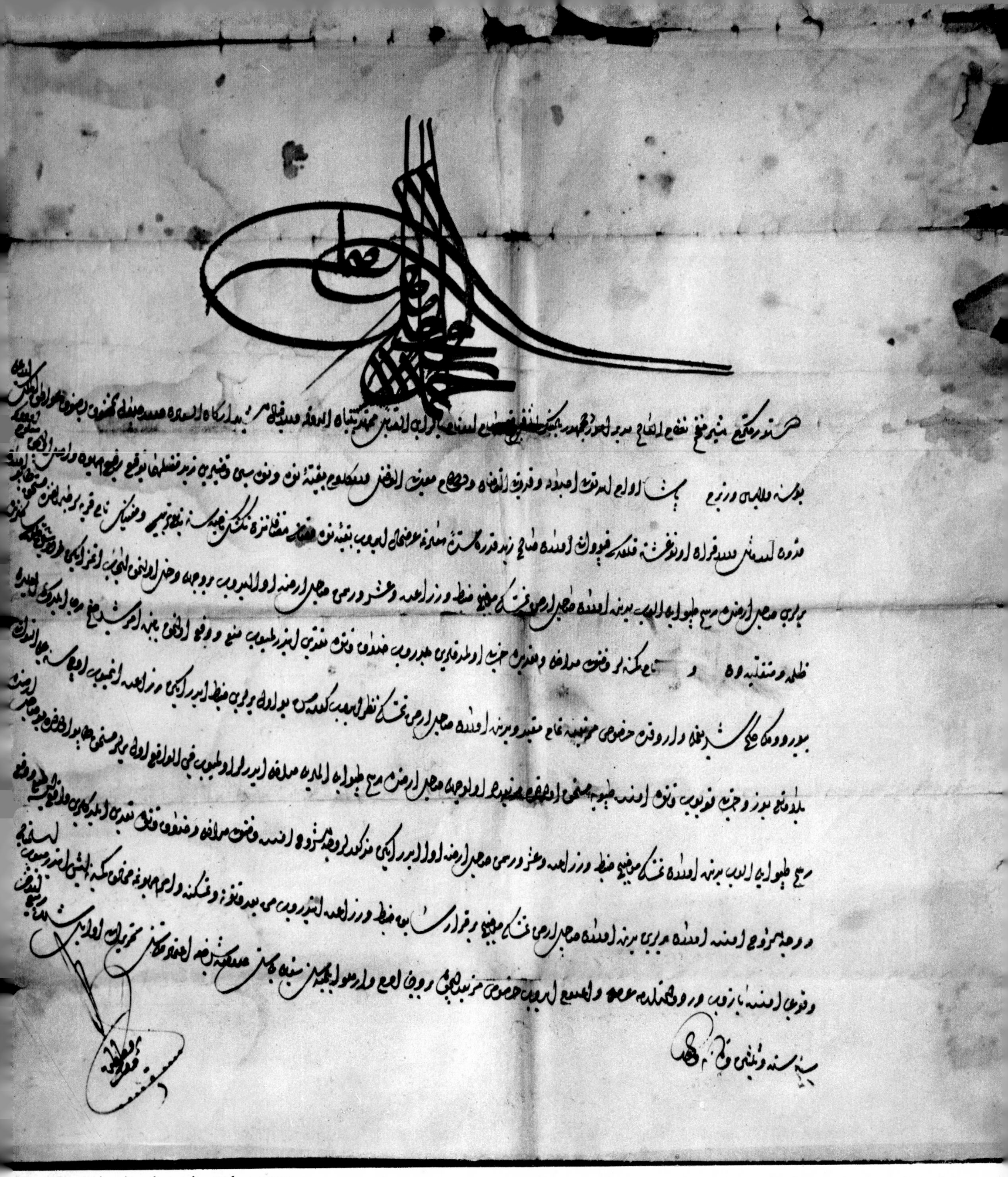

Turkish edict from the 18th century

The Ferhadija Mosque — the pulpit

In popular legends the first belfry and the first clock-tower in Bosnia.

Relief compositions on a wooden cross — Gomionica monastery
Reljefne kompozicije na krstu od drveta — manastir Gomionica

Kastel (castle).

The Shadyrvan (fountain).

The Ferhadija Mosque — interior

Ferhat-Pasha's Mausoleum

Before the lit fuse
of the gun barrel
proud as love
Safikada stands.

On her grave there burns tonight
a candle from Damascus
flickering with the blue flame
of a desert flower

Dušan Mutić

The street that twists in passing round the walls
creeping into the depths of the gates without touching the knocker
suddenly jumped into the semi-darkness on the balcony.

What does the look see, resting
on the semi-opened palm?

DEAD EYES CANNOT SEE

A handsome young man was swallowed
by the Vrbas river, when bathing his horses.
A proud girl bemoaned him,
and besought the willow-trees:
"Oh, my sisters, willow-trees of Vrbas,
bring forth my sweetheart!"
The willow-trees listened to her appeal,
and brought forth the silken boy.

The beautiful girl embraced him,
and cried mournfully and sadly:
"Dark eyes why don't you look at me,
as you used to?
Sweet lips, why don't you kiss me,
as you used to?
White arms, why don't you embrace me,
as you used to?"

Above her a slender cloud unfurled,
and a voice spoke out of the cloud:
"Don't be a fool, pretty girl!
Dead eyes cannot watch you,
as they used to;
dead lips cannot kiss you,
as they used to;
dead arms cannot embrace you,
as they used to."

Shrieked and cried the pretty girl:
"Woe upon me, for God's sake!"
This she uttered, and gave up the ghost.

Folk song

It is superfluous to bear out the spiritual and timely benefit, in fact the indispensability of popular schools; anybody who is clever is convinced of that, and I shall not speak for the few quack sages who want to monopolize science, for they do not read anything and will not want to read this either.

Neither the Turks nor their administration hinder our freedom of learning. Neglect and poverty hinder it! But if we worked harder than we have done so far, and were we greater friends of our people, we could overcome poverty, and this is how:

If we asked the Turkish Devlet (government) in Istambul, they would grant us something from the treasury — to which we contribute the most — for our popular schools; another way are voluntary contributions: there are about 160,000 Christians, and more than 500,000 non-Christians in Bosnia. Now, should each of them give at least twenty paras (some, of course, will give nothing, but there will be others who will give ten times more for this holy work). Well, if everything collected each year were invested at an interest of say 6 per cent, in ten years we would have a considerable principal from which to pay teachers, aid poorer students with books, and send cleverer students to foreign countries to improve their knowledge.

One could say a lot more about this popular enterprise, but I think this will suffice for the native. Let us speculate less and work more, for the wise have said that the mouth gibes and the purse talks; that is why I call, with this letter of mine, upon all Bosnians who love their kinsfolk, of both creeds, to extend their hands and start contributing to this cause. Let a few honest men be found in each town, district and monastery, and let them collect the money and keep it until we agree who will look after it; let them send me the names of donors, and the amount they have contributed; I will print all the names, and amounts, and report all accounts faithfully. As for myself, I promise to give — from the time when this starts with God's help — one thaler yearly for the "principal for popular schools in Bosnia". I would like both non-Christians and Christians to have one principal; however, if we cannot, unfortunately, be united to our common benefit, let the non-Christians collect money for their schools, and the Christians for theirs: if we cannot do as we want, let us do as we can!

Ivan Franjo Jukić (1818—1857)
Popular Schools in Bosnia

Unfolded dowry coffer

Ripe fertile autumn and the past in clogs.

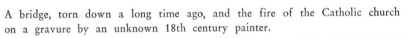

A bridge, torn down a long time ago, and the fire of the Catholic church on a gravure by an unknown 18th century painter.

Market day

Rural motif

National cloth

Rural motif

The Gomionica Nunnery — in 1648 it girdled itself with various dangers, the Matavaz brook, thick walls, honesty of its nuns and its ravens feeding St. Elijah on the frescoes.

The old Orthodox church — Slatina near Banjaluka

The hands are shrewdly picking the small heaps of hope.

Granary

National garb from Zmijanje

In the traces of ancient roads, from wheel to
wheel, the durations of empires are measured.

Italocrytic icon of Our Lady. Distemper on a board 44.5 by 60 cm (16th century, Gomionica monastery)

Italokritska ikona Bogorodice. Tempera na dasci veličine 44,5 × 60 cm (XVI vijek — manastir Gomionica)

Pottery

The tower, Bjelajci

The harvest of fire's and hands' skill.

The scythe rings.

Apparition
of death
I shall give you — life.
I offer you my grave —
for repose.

The Moštanica Monastery, Dubica

Country motif

The Glamoč "kolo" (national dance)

Austrian beach below the Kastel

Between two mosques shops
Took the peasants' scarves from the bosom
untied the knot, and the sweaty dinar.

First train in Banjaluka

Wooden bridge on the Vrbas

Old bus on the Banjaluka — Jajce road (1910)

Our folk, like other folks, often complain of the present and talk about the "good old times". The intelligentsia of the world generally condemns this popular statement that the old times were better than the present "progressive and civilized age". The learned forget the facts on which people rely when speaking thus, which indicate obviously that the people's bemoaning old times is rather appropriate. The folk pay little heed to "cultural facts": railroads, steamships, telegraphs, magnets, telephones, photography, theatres, opera, palaces, large towns, the luxury of the rich, factories, navies, torpedoes, machine guns, complex state and church organizations, etc. They pay little attention to great scientists who write "scientifically" about the law of gravitation, the development of kinds and species, fundamentals of aesthetics, brain reflexes, the Byzantine and gothic style, etc. People are concerned with their material and bodily well-being, and they — therefore — remember with pleasure the times past when they were sturdier and looked better, when they and their neighbours had more cattle, horses, sheep, goats, pigs, fields, etc., when they paid less tax and spent less time in the army, when they could hunt in the hills and on water without any hindrance or tax, when they borrowed and lent food, cattle and money without interest, when they were not surrounded by swarms of spies, clerks and soldiers, when "fashion" and social conventions did not wreck their bodily health and material well-being. Today they are oppressed and drained by all this, and that is why they find the present time bad and worse than the previous, that is why they regret the "good old times". Those times were better for them, although they had less freedom then. The folk, therefore, think well and wisely. They don't want these "cultural facts and freedoms" to bring more taxes, wars, fashions, immorality etc., but an improvement and greater general happiness.

(Vaso Pelagić, Belations Between the Conquerors and the Conquered, Between the Rich and the Poor, up to 1850, published in the book History of the Bosnian-Herzegovinian Uprising, 1879)

TO FREEDOM

Many centuries, many generations and poets have glorified Thee. A lot of fresh blood has been shed for Thee and in Thy name!

From Thy blood-red lips there murmur and flow everlastingly sweet and exultant soul-stirring words that exalt the trampled-down slaves to trembling rapture! Thou, oh pure and bright woman, have begotten from times primordial, and through the deep and infinite eternity your full and exuberant bosom has smelt irresistibly with the passionate and sensual girlhood that enraptures and opiates.

Delighted and carried away by the boiling and endlessly excited blood inherited from my ancestral Balkan rebels, aware — in the vital splendour — of Thy beauty and full lavishness of Thy mercy and power, I — small and insignificant — fall upon my kness before Thee and pray in exaltation to Thee, oh Limitless, oh Endless and Infinite: come at last and visit my country, for everything is nothing without Thee — nothing is everything with Thee! Centuries would darken, peoples would run wild if Thy star did not shine high aloft.

In divine wrath that shakes the universe, come vengefully, with a blood-stained whip in Thy hand, and banish the debauched harlot who has risen — wrapped in the ornate veil of donated rights, under Thy great and sacred name, and with its tainted odour — to Thy radiant and sublime throne in this country of ours!

Let from Thy lips the flame of fire and vengeance and burn, in bitter frenzy, the heinous rakes that serve, basely and cowardly, the venomous harlot! Let sounds of exalted song of effort and strife thunder and echo, oh sublime and godlike woman, from Thy lips red as the heavenly red, through this petrified and ghastly silence!

Shake this stale country, move the frozen hearts, refresh and strengthen them, let everybody and everything feel the immense radiance and charm of beauty, all the lavishness of Thy mercy and power, as they are felt a-trembling by the boiling and ever excited blood of mine, bequeathed me by my ancestral Balkan rebels!

Petar KOČIĆ

From the gentle threshold of the sarcophagus
      where infinity saves those
      whose strength has given out
      and who have been absorbed
            by the dampness
              of universe
  my look, oh gentlest and dear Earth
  leans to your forehead and accepts it.

                    Kolja MIĆEVIĆ

The Orient at Europe's door

The Banjaluka High School

The watches could not catch up with new times

»Balkan« Hotel

Villas

Petrićevac — the Franciscan monastery and church

Interior of the bishop's church

Delibašino Selo — Trappist monastery, and hydro-power station.

ЧЕ ВЗНЕНІА ВЪСЕ РЕ ЛА ПРЗА

НА МАЛЪ Н ВЪРНЫ СТРД
ГЛ҃Ь А҃ . ПО И КСНЫМЪ ТНЮ
ТЫ ЧЛКЮ СОУЩЕСТВЮ
ТЕ СЪ ПАВИЛЪ . ВЪ ПСКОВОЮ
ЮБКОВНІЛЬ ВЪ СЛУГКЛА . Н
ПЛЪТІЮ ВЪ ЗНЕСЕ . СЕ ДЪ
НА ВНСОТЕ СЛОВЕ Б҃ЖІН
ѡ АБСНОУЮ РОДНТЕЛА .
ѧ Ѧ БМ҃ЖЕ НПЛ КЫТЕ КСН
ѡ ОУ МЛІ Ю ВЪ РНЫН НН Е
ВЪ РНЫНМЪ ЧЛЕМЪ :. в҃
А ПЛ҃Ш ВЪ ПЛА҃ОУ Х҃ВЪМ
АГ҃ГЛЫ . МОУ ЖІЕ ГП҃Ш
ЗРА ЩЕ ВЪС ХОДА ЩААГО
ГП҃Ъ Х҃А Ж НЗ НОДАВЦА .
ТА КО ЖЕ Н СОУ Д ІН ВСЕ
МЪ ПРІНД ЕТЬ . ВСЕМЪ
СЫН Б҃ЖЕ . Н ВЪ СЕМЪ
ПОДАЮ АНІЮ СЪ ДЪ ҐГАННАА
Н МАН :.

РЗНЕНІЕМЬ ПР ВОН МЬ
ѡ ЗАР НШЕСЕ ѡ ПСЕ ЧЛ КО
ЛЮБЧЕ . БЕСЪ МРТНЫЕ

Н В҃ЖТ НЫ МЬ ѡ ПО БНЛАСЕ СН
ОЛАВЫ . ѡ ВОНАМЪ ВЪ ЗНЕ
ПІ ЕМЬ С СТРА ШНЫМ ҐБОУ
ЖЛЕСНІМ ТН . А ДЬ ГОТ ПРѢ
ПЕЛИ ВЕ . ѡ ДА РН СРЦА СБОН
ПРОСВ ЩЕНІЕМЬ . Н НАМЬ
ВЪ С ПЪ ГВАЮ ЩНМ ТГ :.
О ЛА . Н НН А . ГЛ҃Ь . ҇е
ПРІНДЕ ТЕ ВЪ ҐРНЫ СБСТН
ПВ ЛЕНІА . ОУ МЪ Г ТА НН О
НА ОУГ НВЪ ЩЕ ОУ ЧЕННКА
Х҃ БЪ ХЪ . НЕ ПР ВЕ СТАН НО
 И КНІЕМЬ РГКЪМЬ . НА
Е ЛЕѡ НСЦЕ И ҐА КО ЖЕ ГА҃А
О ЛА ВДОМЬ ВЪ СЪ Ч ТІ ЕМЬ .
ВЪ ЗА І А Т БЪ ВЪ ВЪ С КЛНКЮ
КЕНІН . ГПЪ ВЫ ГЛА СЪ ТРОУ
БН Ѣ . А ДА І БА ВНТЬ ПѢ ПА
ЛА СЕ НА ЧА ѡ СЪ БЛА ЗНЪ
ВРА ЖІН . Н ПРОСВѢ ТН
ТЬ Д ШЕ НА ШЕ :. Ґ НА СТІВНА
ѡ ТРЫ ГЛ҃Ь . в҃ . ПО ДО МЕ БРА
ҐІО НО КО ЛЪ ПН О . ЧЛ҃КОЕ

Old manuscript, Serbocroatian review (16th century, Gomionica monastery)
Stari rukopis, srpskohrvatska recenzija (XVI vijek, manastir Gomionica)

Lauš mine with power plant

Fra Grga Martić Street

Ferhadija Mosque

Market day

Gornji Šeher

Banski dvori (governor's palaces)

1st May celebration, in 1921, in the Trappist forest near Banjaluka.

Members of the PELAGIĆ Workers' Society and of
the BORAC football club, Banjaluka, 1935

Workers of the Banjaluka waterworks, 1937

Protest meeting of Banjaluka workers in 1939

Youth choir of the PELAGIĆ Society, Banjaluka, in 1940

Slatina — medicinal spring

Strike of the building workers in Banjaluka, 1938

УПРАВА ПОЛИЦИЈЕ БАЊА ЛУКА
   Пов. Бр. 1245/38
28. ј у л а 1938 године
   БАЊА ЛУКА.

Предмет; Штрајк грађевинских радника
        у Бањој Луци.-

            КРАЉЕВСКОЈ БАНСКОЈ УПРАВИ
                  -VI одељењу-

                    БАЊА ЛУКА

        Част ми је известити Краљевску банску Управу, да
су данас 28. овог месеца у 7 часова ујутро грађевински радни-
ци, њих око 450 ступили у штрајк. До штрајка је дошло услед то-
га, што грађевински предузимачи на преговорима код овдашњег
среског Начелства нису пристали на радничке захтеве: установље-
ње 9 часовног радног времена, повишење минималних надница, од-
ређивање плате за квалификоване раднике и помоћно особље од 3½
до 7 динара на сат, да се прековремени рад плаћа 100% скупље,
да се забрани недељни рад и да се забрани сваки акордни рад.

        На дан 27. ов. месеца увече одржана је скупштина
грађевинских радника у овдашњем радничком дому, којој је при-
суствовало око 400 грађевинских радника. Ту су их њихови по-
вереници известили о досадашњем неуспелом преговарању са грађевинским предузимачима по њиховим горњим захтевима, па су је-
дногласно закључили да 28. ов. месеца ступе у штрајк и изабрали
су преговарајући штрајкачки одбор у који су ушли т.Радан Паво зидар. Собо Смаил зидар, Јавић Цветко зидар, Мајић Паво зидар,
Матетић Фрањо зидар, Тухтан Иво зидар, Јурић Мато зидар, Кир-
тнер Ђуро тесар, Мијатовић Анто радник и Шабић Иван радник сви
из Бања Луке, који ће водити даље преговоре са грађевинским
предузимачима по напред изведеним радничким захтевима.

        Скупштина је протекла у потпуном реду и присутни су
се мирно разишли.

                        Зам. Управника полиције
                        Виши полиц. комесар,

                            Арвајлар

In the period between the two wars a wide and extensive discussion took place on the responsibility for World War One. The question: who is guilty? also interested the masses, and so the investigation came under the control of the people who wanted to know why they had fought and why a war was being prepared again. The question of responsibility for the past war, and the question of responsibility for the new one, thus became a practical political issue, and it is therefore obvious why countless books have been devoted to the subject in all countries.

In this enormous literature, a very important place is that of military responsibility with regard to the assassination of the Archduke in Sarajevo, this being the only item of interest for us here.

*

*   *

Without dwelling on opinions that have nothing to do with the investigation of war responsibility in view of its direct relation with the killing, or on the opinion — sanctioned by the Versailles Peace Treaty — regarding the exclusive responsibility of Germany, we nevertheless have to sketch a view which — although not developed in connection with the Sarajevo affair — permits a proper and full understanding of the true relation of the event to all those causes that brought about the world war. This is an opinion* which holds that war is the result of imperialist contrasts which are evidenced all over the world, and that the matter of military responsibility is not, therefore, a question involving the responsibility of a specific government, and even less of a man or of an act. This opinion is the result of the scientific analysis of the modern development of capitalism, and it established — much before the War actually broke out — that there had to be a war, and that wars would occur for as long as there were imperialist contrasts since these could not be solved otherwise in the clash between the interested imperialisms. Wars are fought for a new division of the world which — even if it were new after a war (which was not the case after World War One) — could not solve the problem permanently. With this and such approach to the problem, this opinion implicitly rejects the thesis about the responsibility of those who shot the Archduke for the World War.

---

* Here Masleša thought of Lenin, of his analysis of imperialism as the last stage of capitalism.

However, even if such a view establishes war responsibility on a world-wide scale, and uncovers the essence of the problems underlying the causes of war and determines its social responsibilities, one cannot obliterate the historic existence of the Sarajevo assassination, or the fact that it is linked with the date of beginning of the World War.

*

* *

This brief methodological and abstract critique of the various investigations and views on the causes of the war in connection with the Sarajevo assassination should also be explained and shown historically. Thus, we shall be able to understand properly the action of the Mlada Bosna Movement in the international economic and political situation of the time, and only then will the international importance of a revolutionary action, at a time of major and poignant imperialists contrasts, be fully understood.

*

* *

We have seen how the problem of imperialist contrarieties — from worldwide differences in the search for the most favourable solution, in fact for solutions in stages — boiled down to the Balkans and, ever further, to the inner consolidation and strengthening of Austro-Hungary, in which Bosnia played an important role as political and strategic point; we have also seen its comeback to the point of departure after its opening. In a moment of history the fight for the colonies became the fight for Bosnia and Herzegovina, and the fight for Bosnia got its true meaning through the fight for colonies and world supremacy.

In that respect, and only in that respect, the Sarajevo assassination, as a part of the fight for Bosnia, really is one of the causes of the War, and it is those who led this fight for Bosnia that are responsible for the War, not the followers of the Mlada Bosna who wanted free and independent Bosnia and Herzegovina regardless of any imperialist interest.

Veselin Masleša (1906—1943), fragments from the study The Mlada Bosna Movement and Question of War Responsibility

The "black house", the prison of the patriots and revolutionaries of the Krajina Region.

Orthodox church

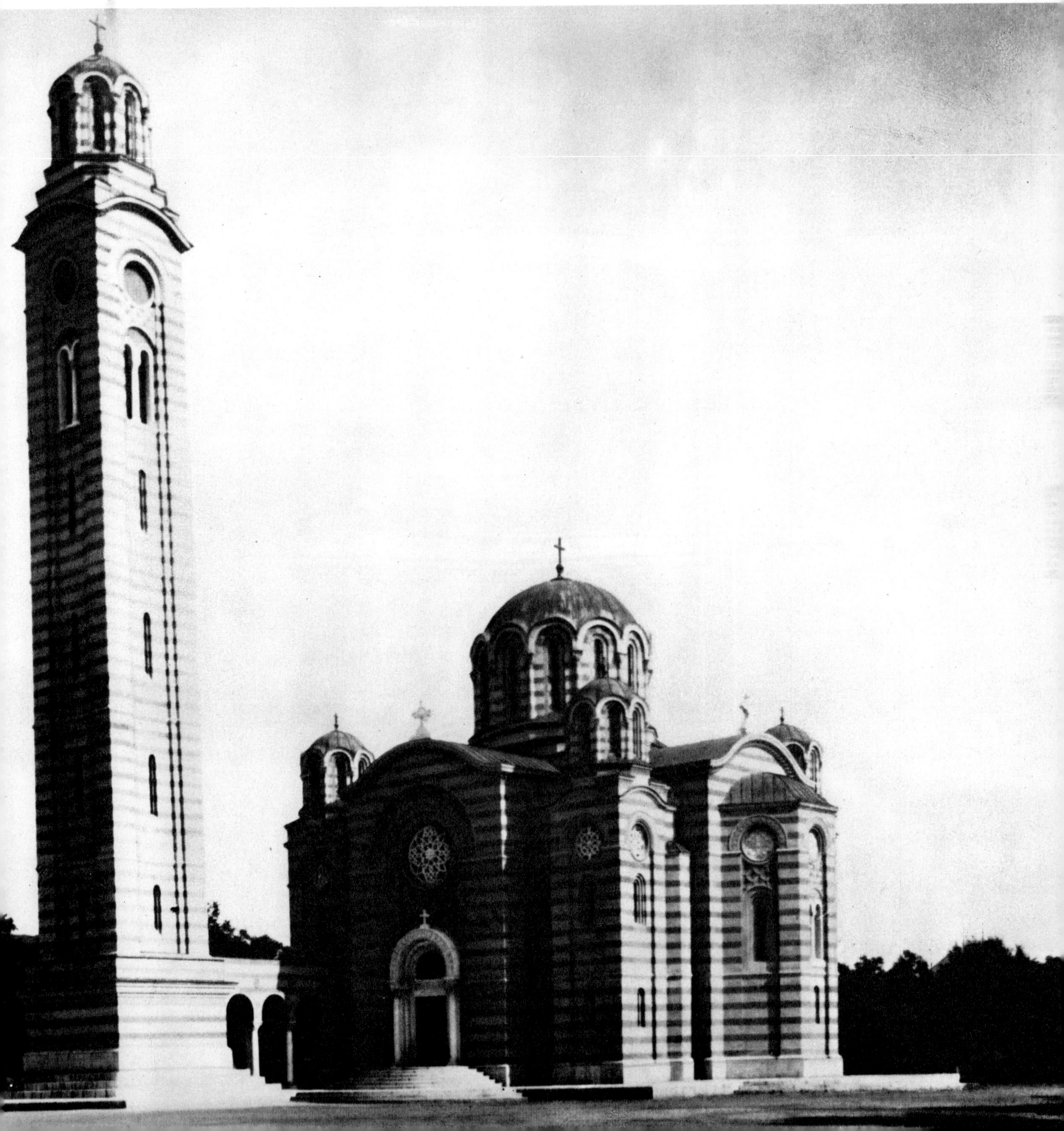

Špiro Bocarić
(1878—1941)
Girl at the fountain

The National Theatre of the Krajina Region.

Hypothecary Bank

HANDS ON THE ALTAR

Don't call me, don't call, tonight, from behind the hill, my friend
I am tired of walking, I am dead of penury.

As a wedding party of woe, the winds moan on the slopes:
darkness covers my traces.
Blood boils from the wounds
and circles round me knee-deep.

I am silent, for sleep will maybe come on the roads of no faith:
I lay my pale hands on the altar of cold waste land;
the gloomy hours creep like snakes through the rot of my lungs;
my devote silence deafens pace and sound,
my great penury deafens hunger and lament.

It is far to dawn, far to resurrection!
Darkness covers my traces.
Blood boils from the wounds.
The altar is cold. My hands are cold.
I am silent and awake.

Mile BEKUT (1915—1933)

Antun Augustinčić, Monument of Petar Kočić (1932)

The workers' movement in Banjaluka and the Bosanska Krajina region, its development, inner turmoil and growth in pre-war Yugoslavia (1918—1941), is an integral part of the general struggle of the working class of Yugoslavia for its rights, and against capitalist exploitation and national oppression. In the single stages of its growth, this struggle assumed varying aspects and forms, but it was always marked by its class-oriented character.

The common Yugoslav state was created in 1918 in an undemocratic way and on undemocratic foundations. The newly-created state did not become a community of equal and free people and — in the very beginning — the monarchy and the bourgeoisie showed that they would care only for their own interests. The masses of workers and farmers, under the burden of the economic crisis and political rightlessness, again started struggling for their rights, and better working and living conditions. The contrasts in which the Kindgom of Serbs, Croats and Slovenes was created were very soon reflected on the life of Banjaluka and of the Bosanska Krajina. The revolutionary and militant attitude of the workers, influenced considerably by the history of the October Revolution in Russia, intimidated the bourgeoisie, and it constantly kent a vigilant eye on the trends in the workers' movement, mobilizing against it all administrative and police bodies, and even military units.

Because of the workers' rebellious mood on the eve of the First May celebration in 1919, at the order of the Regional Government for Bosnia and Herzegovina the authorities in Banjaluka introduced martial law; it authorized the court-martial to kill any citizen, without trial, who would show any kind of dissatisfaction with the system.

Bourgeoisie's violent harassment of the working class did not suppress its fighting spirit, but strengthened it even more. 1919 and 1920 were a period of major and successful actions of the political and trade union workers' organizations throughout the Bosanska Krajina region, and Banjaluka became the revolutionary centre from which many actions in the region were directed and led. At the time, active in the town were the Regional Committee of the Communist Party of Yugoslavia, the Local Committee of the Communist Party of Yugoslavia, the Local Trade Union Council, the Workers' Hall, the Workers' Consumer Co-operative, the evening political school, the workers' cinema Union. In the spring of 1920, Glas Naroda (Voice of the People), newspaper of the communist party of Yugoslavia, came out of print. Its articles mobilized working class and informed the public about the actual political situation. The communist party representative won the elections for the constituent assembly in the autumn in 1920. This electoral victory reflected the trust of the public in Banjaluka and its environs in the programme of the communist party of Yugoslavia, established at the historical congress of the party in Vukovar.

The powerful revolutionary upheavals in the entire country, the political victories of the communist party of Yugoslavia during elections, the mass revival of strikes, and other political manifestations of organized workers' movement, forced bourgeoisie to speed up the implementation of measures with which it wanted to repulse the revolutionary workers' movement. With the "Obznana", the so-called Vidovdan Constitution, and Law on the Protection of the State, the ruling class prohibited the activity of the communist party of Yugoslavia, and started taking its revenge — through the grossest violence — upon the revolutionary workers' movement.

In the very difficult conditions of persecution and violence, the party began to organize underground party cells throughout the country. Thus, illegal local organizations of the communist party of Yugoslavia and of the communist youth of Yugoslavia were formed in Banjaluka too at the time. The communists — workers and intellectuals alike — created a unique front of struggle, established societies and organized numerous actions through the trade unions. Among the most outstanding political workers in Banjaluka were (at the time) Pavao Radan, mason, and Akif Šeremet, professor at the Banjaluka High School. The links between the communist party organization and the progressive forces in Banjaluka permitted large-scale political action to the working class. The fruit of such activities was — among others — the foundation of the Workers' Sports Society Borac (the fighter) in 1925, and of the Workers' Cultural-Sports Society Pelagić in 1927. During that period the trade union movement developed more rapidly, and new organizations were established with communists at their head. Under their leadership, the trade union shops took active part in the protection of the workers' political and economic rights, and in the creation of united militant unions.

The Fourth Congress of the Communist Party of Yugoslavia was held in the autumn of 1928 in Dresden. It was attended by 22 delegates from Yugoslavia, including the delegate of the Banjaluka party organization.

Radničko kulturno društvo „PELAGIĆ" B. Luka

priređuje u subotu 11 o. m. u 9 sati na veče
U PROSTORIJAMA HRVATSKOG DOMA

RADNIČKO KULTURNO VEČE

sa igrankom

NA PROGRAMU JE:

I Dio

Blobner:	**Radnički pozdrav**	
Friodina:	Ah ti stepj širokaja	pjeva zbor „Pelagića"
* . *	Slobodnjačka	
Čmelov:	Veseli kovači Kuznjeca	

II dio

Jegor Bulyčov, drama od Maksima Gorkog izvode članovi
diletantske sekcije „Pelagića"

III dio

Schubert:	**Uspavanka**, izvodi muzička sekcija „Pelagića"	
Toller :	**Pjesma banjolučkih radnika**	pjeva zbor „Pelagića" uz pratnju orkestra muzičke sekcije
Dunajevski:	**Zapjevaj pjesmu**	
Dunajevski:	**Pjesma besprizornih**	
Davidenko:	**Konjička**	
* . *	**Naša pjesma**	

Radnici izlaze pred javnost, da pokažu prijateljima radničkog pokreta, svima prijateljima kulture i napretka, svoj trud na kulturnom radu i **da dokažu svima da je jedina radnička klasa sposobna da daje kulturne vrijednosti**, da ona to hoće, i da to mora, ako hoće da ima bolji život.

Sa programom kulturne večeri, punim poleta i bodrosti, dokazaće da se luč znanja i kulture nalazi u pravim i čvrstim rukama. Sa radničkom i omladinskom pjesmom, sa istinsk m životom radnika datim na pozornici sa ozbiljnom riječi i zdravim veseljem snažne radničke klase pronijeće luč duhovnog svjetla u zamračene radničke izbe, uvijene u bijedu i patnju, osvijetliće plamenim sjajem nastojanja radnika za ljepšim životom i uzbuditi srca svima iskrenim prijateljima napretka.

Danas, kada bjesni imperijalistički rat, a kapitalisti se kockaju sa tekovinama kulture, kada se sav teret bijede i nedaća podvostručio na plećima radnoga svijeta, kada je i poslednja rupa na kaišu ostala široka, jer je glad zamjenila nadu na bolje, kada glad i krv radnika, zanatlije ili radnog inteligenta nosi zlato špekulantima, krupnim liferantima i trgovcima, osjeća se potreba za znanjem više nego ikada.

Danas, kada su sve tekovine tako zvane zapadne civilizacije otkazale svoju primjenu za dobro čovječanstva, kada uništavanja kulturnih vrijednosti znače pobjedu a uništavanje čovjeka postaje ciljem osjeća se potreba prave kulture više nego ikada.

Radničko kulturno društvo „Pelagić" poziva sve prijatelje kulture, mira i napretka, sve radnike i radnice i svu slobodarsku javnost da doprinesu svoj dio naporima radničke klase za kulturniji, ljepši i bolji život, da svojom posjetom dadu moralnu podršku tim naporima i omoguće dalji plodni kulturni rad onima kojima je znanje i kultura najpotrebnija.

Radničko kulturno društvo
„Pelagić"

Nakladnik: SLOBODAN KOKANOVIĆ

With the onset of the "January 6" dictatorship in 1929, the bourgeoisie and the monarchy again began to attack the workers' movement throughout the country. In Banjaluka they closed down the Workers' Hall, impounded party property and files, and started persecuting the most outstanding worker leaders.

Despite the exceptionally difficult conditions, during the very same years young and fighting communists appeared in the political life of Banjaluka. They developed new forms of political activity which influenced the further development of the revolutionary workers' movement. The third conference of the party organization in Banjaluka, held in 1934, decided to start political activity on a large-scale basis. In August, 1934, the KAB (Club of Academicians of Banjaluka) was founded: the club, and its programme, rallied progressive intellectuals and students. Under the leadership of communists, the KAB extended its activities, united the work of young workers, high school and university students introducing, thus, new powerful impulses into the political life of the Bosanska Krajina region.

At the May 5, 1935 elections, the dictatorship had to withdraw before the growing pressure of national resistance and of the workers' movement.

In June of the same year the Banjaluka communists and activists of the revolutionary workers' movement started publishing the Narodna Pravda (National Justice) newspaper. From the very first issue the paper gained full political recognition in the country. It exercised a powerful political influence on the farmers, and brought rural population into closer contact with the programme of the communist party of Yugoslavia. These were reasons why the police prohibited further issue and impounded the fifth (and last) number. The numerous and mass actions of the workers' movement began to assume, more and more, legal forms of struggle. The communists in the Pelagić, Nature's Friend and KAB societies worked even more successfully on bringing together the town and the country, especially in the Banjaluka district.

The further development of social and political activity continued in spite of the betrayal — in 1936 — of the Banjaluka party organization and the arrest of several outstanding communists and labour leaders. In that period, the party organization of Banjaluka also had to struggle against the faction which was trying to prevent the accepted course of gaining political strength in socio-political institutions and organizations for which the Party fought and through which it exercised its political influence. Thanks, first of all, to the political and ideological influence of the party on the workers, students and intellectuals, the faction was politically and ideologically very soon eliminated from the workers' movement. This ideological and political settlement created conditions for an even faster development of the movement.

In the period from 1937 to 1941, after Josip Broz Tito took over the helm of the party, large-scale work developed in Banjaluka and in the Bosanska Krajina region on the rallying of all progressive forces round the programme of the communist party of Yugoslavia. The development of the workers' movement in this period was marked by the Party's most successful and widest influence on socio-political life in Banjaluka and the Bosanska Krajina. Through a number of manifestations and political actions, organized by the party, freedom-loving Banjaluka and Bosanska Krajina provided their own contribution to the struggle against the fascization of Yugoslavia.

Numerous strikes were organized all over the Bosanska Krajina region, especially in Banjaluka, Drvar, Ljubija, Prijedor and Bihać. A great many of these ended with the victory of the workers who were supported, in their struggle, by all democratic people.

The workers' organization of Banjaluka and elsewhere took active part in political actions organized by the Party to aid the republicans in Spain.

The 1938 elections in Banjaluka were marked by an even stronger confrontation of political forces, and by the increased rallying of democratic forces round the Communist Party of Yugoslavia, which set up its own candidate at the elections.

When Hitler occupied Czechoslovakia, the Banjaluka party organization organized mass demonstrations in which several thousand citizens took part, carrying antifascist slogans and voicing their protest. The demonstrations organized by the communists on the occasion of the Congress of Yugoslav Techers in Banjaluka were another contribution to the further blazing of antifascist struggle. In these and many other demonstrations and manifestations of the freedom-loving spirit, the workers and students of Banjaluka were in the front ranks, together with all democratic forces, providing their own contribution to the struggle against fascism. This led to the final showdown between the progressive and democratic youth and the fascist organizations of the "ljo-tićevci" and "frankovci". The fight, led in the streets and within the organizations of high school and university students, was won entirely by the progressive youth movement.

The powerful growth of revolutionary forces followed the performances of the Workers' Cultural Society Pelagić in almost every town and village in the Bosanska Krajina. In Jajce, Bihać, Bosanska Krupa, Drvar and Teslić the performances by this society became, as a rule, great political meetings. All police attempts to prevent the activity of the Pelagić Society — prohibiting the performances, arresting the society's leaders, and even stopping the trains by which the members of the society travelled — failed.

In late 1940 and early 1941 the authorities took more severe steps against the freedom-loving forces and the workers' movement; the work of the United Workers' Trade Union Association, KAB, Pelagić, Borac and all other organizations through which the revolutionary movement acted, was forbidden. Outstanding party members were arrested and interned in concentration camps. However, the revolutionary movement only gained impetus, and no terror or prohibitions could stop it any longer.

Through its high and low tides, ascents and declines, from 1919 to 1941, the revolutionary workers' movement of Banjaluka and of the Bosanska Krajina region met the historical events of 1941 well-organized, united and militant. Its long activity tempered a great number of revolutionary fighters who — enriched with their fighting experience, in the decisive battles of the uprising and revolution, in Banjaluka, in the Bosanska Krajina, and on fronts all over the country — gave an important contribution to the general victory of our peoples against the fascist invaders and native traitors.

Immediately after the occupation of the country, Banjaluka became the headquarters of the ustaše military staff and of a stronger garrison of German occupying troops. All legal forms of political life in the town were forcefully interrupted. Except the ustaše movement, no other party could appear any longer on the political stage. Particularly violent attacks were directed at the unity of the masses which had been attained — especially in the years preceding the outbreak of war — within the struggle of the workers' movement and people's front for democratic freedom, against the fascization of the country, and for defense from foreign fascist danger.

The rule set down by the invaders and quislings was directed at breaking this unity, on a religious and national basis, with the threatening policy of fratricidal war.

From the very onset, the German invader struck upon the Serbian part of the population. For any breach of the rules of the occupying authorities or of order the culprit was sought, and hostages taken, exclusively among the Serbs. This part of the population was practically outlawed by the ustaše authorities, as nazism did with the Jews. As opposed to that, the invader tried not to cause a feeling of insecurity among the Croatian and Moslem part of the population, while the propaganda of the ustaše did everything to present the creation of the quisling Independent Croatian State (Nezavisna Država Hrvatska, NDH) as the realization of the centuries-long aspirations of the Croats and Moslems. However, the pogrom policy of the ustaše and the occupying military policy of the Germans could not but cause a feeling of heavy doubt regarding their ultimate intentions, and a deep concern with the state of affairs, even in that part of the population. The very fact that the tragedy of the Serbian people took place before their eyes, and that the armed forces of the NDH were forcefully recruited from among the Croats and Moslems, in the middle of an international war the outcome and end of which could not be seen, brought peace and tranquility to nobody. Thus, the general situation in Banjaluka and the Bosanska Krajina took a tragic turn.

Complete insecurity spread: the measures taken by the occupying and ustaše authorities were followed with fear. Everybody was aware of the coming evil which could not be stopped.

The occupation of the country and the appearance of the darkest forces on the political scene meant moments of great national trial, when even the ballast of the dark side of the past could assume unthought-of dimensions. The call of the Communist Party of Yugoslavia to the struggle gave the communists of the Bosanska Krajina the vision of a different outcome, which they trusted deeply, and which filled them with the self-confidence to live and act in the extraordinary circumstances.

2

In the new circumstances of the war and occupation, the attitude of the Communist Party of Yugoslavia remained as unambiguous and clear as ever. On April 10, 1941, while the Yugoslav army was falling apart, the Political

Bureau of the Central Committee pointed out, to all communists, the importance of preserving the party's organizational unity, of escaping captivity, and hiding all arms they could lay their hands on. At the same time, a military committee, led by Tito, was established within the Central Committee of the party. On April 15, while the country was being divided, and the quisling Independent Croatian State (NDH) founded, the proclamation of the Central Committee called everybody to keep resisting the invader, pointing out that the communists and the workers' class would be the "in the first ranks of the struggle against the invader" and that they would endure in that struggle "to final victory"; in the May 1 proclamation the Central Committee pointed out that that party would "even more persistently organize and lead the fight against the occupying forces and national traitors, against the stirring of national hatred, and for the brotherhood of the peoples of Yugoslavia and all nations on the Balkan peninsula." At the May consultation of the Communist Party of Yugoslavia it was decided to form military committees in every party committee, and to start accepting new party members. On the day of German onslaught on the Soviet Union, the Political Bureau of the Central Committee issued a proclamation to the workers' class and to the peoples of Yugoslavia, calling them to assist with all means the just struggle of the Soviet Union for it was also their own. On July 12 the Central Committee, on the basis of its July 4 decision, called all Yugoslav peoples to turn their country into a besieged fortress for the fascist invaders, and called all communists to organize, without delay, partisan units and to lead the people's liberation war. Because of all that, at that time the links between party organizations and leading bodies were of vital importance.

The liaison between the party organizations in the Bosanska Krajina and the regional party leadership in Banjaluka was fully provided for. Of course, it could not be organized on an everyday, but on a periodical basis, but it was accurate and functional. Through this channel the party units in the field were supplied with the most necessary party material, information on the situation in the country and in the world, and received orders of a military nature. In that respect of particular importance were the regional party meeting on the Šehitluci hill above Banjaluka, the regional meetings in Orlovci above Prijedor, in Osmača, and elsewhere.

Thanks to its readiness, politically the party in the Bosanska Krajina was ready to meet the turn of events, and the alertness among the membership of some of its units (Drvar, Kozara) was transmitted almost to all the people. Of course, the party organization could not put a stop to the crimes of the occupying army and of the ustaše, especially not in the beginning. However, as soon as it had gained political control over the situation, while preparing armed resistance in single areas, it could follow closely and thwart in time every infernal plan of the enemy. Consequently, after the first crimes committed all over the Krajina, the ustaše and the occupying forces did not succeed in continuing the policy of extermination of the Serbian population.

As soon as the party organization in the Bosanska Krajina started to follow the line of armed struggle of the Communist Party of Yugoslavia, the number of its members grew, and the network of its units spread. The turning point in this direction was the large-scale work of the communists, members of the communist youth organization, their followers and leaders, who left the occupied towns for the Krajina villages. That was, actually, the beginning of mass political work of the communists in the Krajina villages, and of the party's organizational strengthening in them. The Banjaluka party organization played an especially important part in those activities. It was the most numerous organization, and its members were distributed everywhere, all over the territory of the Bosanska Krajina: in the Kozara and Podgrmeč areas, central Bosnia, the areas round Jajce, Ključ, Petrovac, and Drvar. With such work the Banjaluka unit continued, in the most consistent manner, its rich revolutionary activity at the most crucial time.

At the time, the military organization of the party became the backbone of the life and work of the party organization in the Bosanska Krajina. In May and first half of June party members listed all available arms and ammunition so that the party knew what it had on hand; by the end of June the party established a network of military commissioners, through whom the party gained the first information on the number of people ready and able to start armed resistance; in the latter half of July district military staffs were organized, and the first military units created — detachments, companies and groups. In this way, in about two months' time the military organization was ready for all forms of armed struggle.

In the beginning, the communists had to start armed resistance through sabotage groups, who carried out unremitting attacks on the occupying forces' arms, ammunition, fuel, and food depots in the occupied towns, mined bridges, demolished railways, defended villages from the ustaše onslaughts, etc.

They believed sincerely, especially after Germany's attack on the Soviet Union, that such sabotage actions would create an unbearable situation for the invader and force him to bring ever new reinforcements, which would make him weaker on the world front where the fate was being decided.

However, through their work among the people the communists of the Bosanska Krajina understood, at the proper time, that mass armed struggle — in which sabotage and other forms of fighting the enemy could be used according to circumstances — was the only alternative for the Serbs who found themselves in the quisling Croatian state (Bosnia and Herzegovina, Lika, Kordun, Banija), especially after the massacres carried out by the ustaše, when it became clear that the only answer was war against the puppet state and the German invader. The communists saw clearly that only such struggle could show promise also for the Croatian and Moslem part of the population. That meant that only the strength of general resistance could put a stop to the sown illusions and to the tendency of conciliation with the occupation. Only such a struggle could help the people to retain their moral integrity, which had existed before the occupation and which had persisted throughout the activity of the workers' movement and people's front in Banjaluka and all over the Bosanska Krajina. By the composition of their organization, the Bosanska Krajina dommunists were the most politically conscious and the most militant part of the Serbian, Croatian and Moslem people, and that is why they were able to express — in the decisive moment — the fighting tradition of all these peoples. The idea of common struggle, of brotherhood and unity were the topmost tasks of political action of the communists at a time when the Bosanska Krajina was on the brim of fratricidal war. They were equal to their task, for they did not regard armed struggle as a play of circumstances, but as a historical turning point, at which the movement of the masses had its own growth, period of maturity, and its relentless inner laws of motion.

3

Armed struggle began in the southwestern part of the Bosanska Krajina. Having known the situation in its area and, first of all, its own force and the disposition of the people, the enemy's strength, the military-political leadership of the Bosansko Grahovo district decided to attack the ustaše garrison in Drvar. The decision was also influenced by the liaison of this staff with the military-political leaderships in the districts of Bosanski Petrovac and Glamoč, and in Lika. That provided for the simultaneous outbreak of the uprising in the entire southwestern part of the Bosanska Krajina and in Lika, and the concurrent liberation of Drvar, Bosansko Grahovo, Oštrelj and Srb on July 27, 1941.

Ever since its beginning, the armed struggle of our peoples was an unequal one, and its absolute rule was not to retain the occupied stronghold or territory at any cost, and to avoid frontal confrontation with the military--technically superior adversary.

In the southwestern part of the Bosanska Krajina and in Lika the resistance forces were even for a time militarily superior, with 4,000 armed fighters. Having evaluated their possibilities realistically, the military-political leaders in the area decided to hold the liberated territory through offensive action, and considered it as a whole. Thanks to such a strategy, the armed forces of the NDH not only failed to recapture Drvar, Bosansko Grahovo, Oštrelj and Srb, but also suffered huge losses elsewhere in the Bosanska Krajina, so that they eventually had to reconcile themselves to the Italians occupying the territory.

After the liberation of Drvar, the general uprising started, almost simultaneously, in all the other parts of the Bosanska Krajina — Podgrmeč, Kozara, central Bosnia, Manjača, Pljeva, Janje, Ključ, Cazin. It became the common reality of all these parts of the region, in spite of their entirely different features.

Since practically everybody stood up in arms, and the supply of fire-arms was relatively limited, the fighting units were very heterogeneous. In most cases, the units were organized into guerilla detachments, companies, platoons, squads, sabotage groups. However, all these units were quite capable of attaining the following success in about ten days: they liberated an 80 kilometre long and 25 kilometre wide settled territory on the slopes of the Grmeč mountain, established a front in front of the Potkozarje villages from Bosanski Novi, through Prijedor to Bosanska Dubica and Gradiška; in the immediate nearness of the strong enemy garrison in Banjaluka they smashed every ustaše stronghold; in broad daylight, they attacked the garrison in Skender-Vakuf; all over the Bosanska Krajina they destroyed almost every gendarmerie and ustaše post. Those were times when the occupied Krajina towns — Bosanska Dubica, Bosanska Krupa, Bosanski Petrovac — were stormed several times in a row by the sheer force of the human mass and not by the force of arms; when the Krajina townlets of Bosanska Kostajnica, Glamoč, Mrkonjić were liberated for two or three days at a time; when the Lješljani mine was disabled to the end of the war; when — all over the region — railways and roads were destroyed, enemy troop trucks ambushed, telephone posts torn down; under the nose of enemy garrisons, partisan units destroyed power stations, waterworks; out of the entire occupied territory, actually occupied were only the surrounded garrisons in the Krajina townlets. "Prijedor is surrounded for all the villages have revolted (men, women, children, everybody able to carry a weapon). Send urgent infantry and aircraft reinforcements" (despatch sent from Prijedor to Zagreb on July 31, 1941). Such an overall mass resistance lasted for two full months, until the occupation of Drvar by the Italian occupying troops.

In the military-political sense, the uprising represented only one way of the beginning of armed struggle, of the revolution. In some areas it was, perhaps, the only and the true form. Elsewhere the resistance involved mass sabotages by numerous sapper groups, or partisan detachments, or — in some cases — persevering and patient political activity among the people. Through its patient political action, the party organization in occupied Banjaluka included the people into a widespread liberation movement, which was essentially an integral part of the partisan background, and from which the ranks of partisan troops and of the people's liberation army were continuously filled to the very end of the war.

In the beginning of the uprising the people's army acted, as a rule, through its elementary forms — basic fighting units, through which the people fulfilled their fighting initiative directly. However, despite their initiative and fighting spirit, these units remained small. Depending on circumstances, the basic units could not always be united into larger formations under a single command; likewise, the fundamental bodies of new authority could not always be united into higher ones, especially were the development of the movement surpassed the organizational abilities of its ideological promoters. The question arose, therefore, how to overcome, in the framework of the general fighting activity of the people, the difficulties created by the too small and too numerous units. That became even more necessary after the imminent withdrawal of četnik military organizations from the resistance forces, and in view of the inevitable clash with četnik ideology which was based — from the very first days of the uprising — on retaliation over the Croatian and Moslem part of the population rather than on the fight against the invader.

The reorganization of the resistance forces — army, background and party — which started in October 1941 and ended with the regional party consultation in Skender-Vakuf, in February 1942, had a strategic character and marked a new phase in the development of the people's liberation war in the Bosanska Krajina.

4

The process of overcoming the heterogeneity, first of all of the army, started in the Kozara area in August 1941, with a deliberate, organized and decisive renouncing of frontal struggle, and through the uniting of the heterogeneous resistance forces into three well-armed companies who began to lead a military life. That was also the beginning of systematic and organized socio--political life both in the troops and in the background. The later developments confirmed that such a line was appropriate. The fighting capacity of the Kozara companies was first proved in three successful battles (Podgradci, Turjak, Mrakovica).

The Kozara experience was precious for general reorganization, which proved to be difficult since heterogeneity was the general phenomenon and situation resisting any change. Such a state of affairs and mentality was also favoured by the elementary forms (cells) of the party organization in the Bosanska Krajina, while the district leading bodies acted on too limited areas in order to become promoters of development, especially where the army was involved. Owing to the nature of the uprising, the members of the regional party committee were not together either since the beginning of armed struggle. They were everywhere — in the field, working on operations involving entire areas, and all of Bosanska Krajina. That was why the reorganization involved the troops, the background and the party alike.

Large military formations were created by the time of the Skender--Vakuf consultation: five Krajina people's liberation partisan detachments, consisting of full battalions, both equipment and men-wise. The battalions were organized after a strictly military pattern, and consisted of companies, platoons and squads, including all other auxiliary military units. From September to December, a network of vilage and communal people's liberation committees was formed all over the territory. Of especial importance was the formation of the five district committees of the Communist Party of Yugoslavia. Thus, the party organization reorganized its own network (along with the reorganization in the army, the promoter of which the party actually was) both in the military units and in the background. At the Skender-Vakuf meeting, after the summing-up of the results, the Operations Staff for the Bosanska Krajina was formed, and the district party committee. With such an organization and success in the battlefield, already attained by the partisan detachments, the people's liberation movement had to face, politically, the ideology and the military units of the četniks who started fighting the movement, having relied first of all on the Italians, and then having entered into an agreement with the ustaše and Germans.

For the People's Liberation Movement, the četniks were first of all political adversaries whose ideology was directed at impairing the fighting spirit of the Serbian masses, and at turning these masses against the people's liberation movement when the struggle began to assume large proportions. The outcome of the fight against the četniks was vitally affected by the military success of the 1st, 2nd and 5th Krajina People's Liberation Detachments, which operated in areas where the četniks had no influence at all since the beginning (Kozara), and areas where their appearance was liquidated in time (Podgrmeč, south-western part of the Bosanska Krajina). The liberation of Prijedor and Ljubija on May 15 and 16, 1942, started the irresistible charges of the Krajina partisans against the enemy garrisons, and the liberation of a number of towns in the first half of 1942 (Bosanska Krupa, Ključ, Bosanski Petrovac, Drvar, Glamoč). The decisive showdown with četnik ideology, in spite of the difficulties involved, took place relatively early, in the second year of the war (1942). That won, essentially, the battle for the unity of the Serbian people and for their full support of the People's Liberation Movement in its endeavours to attain the brotherhood and unity of Serbs, Croats and Moslems. And that unity was the basic condition for the successful completion of the struggle against the invader, and the pledge for the foundation of the republic of Bosnia and Herzegovina in new Yugoslavia.

5

The occupying troops and the armed forces of the NDH (Independent Croatian State) in the Bosanska Krajina were reinforced throughout the war, depending on the actual military and political situation, and especially when offensive actions were planned against the liberated territory. When the uprising started, in Bosanska Krajina there were two "domobrani" (regular army) regiments, one ustaše battalion, three gendarmerie regiments, and ustaše garrisons in every town. The very first operation, aimed at the suppression of the uprising, engaged 22 ustaše-domobrani battalions, numerous units of the local ustaše police, parts of a German division with artillery, armour and aircraft support.

Kladuša

Dvor...na

Bos. Novi

KOZARA

Cazin

Ostrožac

Prijedor

Benakovac

Banja Luka

Vrba...

...ihać

GRMEČ

Sanski Most

Udbina

Bos Petrovac

Ključ

Drvar

Jaj...

SLOBODNA TERITORIJA
KRAJINE, NOVEMBRA
1942.

Kupres

Knin

Novska PSUN...

One Italian division, one Italian regiment and 7 ustaše-domobrani battalions tried to suppress the uprising in the southwestern part of Bosanska Krajina, when Drvar, Grahovo and Oštrelj were occupied. In late 1941, the Second Krajina Partisan Detachment on the Kozara was attacked by two reinforced domobrani infantry divisions, a German legion regiment, parts of a German infantry division, ustaše and gendarmerie units — a total of 5,000 soldiers. The famous Second Offensive on the Kozara was launched by 14 German battalions, 25 ustaše and domobrani battalions, 100 guns, several plane squadrons, and 5 Hungarian river monitors, against 5 battalions (3,500 fighters) of the Second Krajina People's Liberation Detachment. That was one of the most unequal fights in the whole People's Liberation War, and major losses and hardships of the soldiers and refugees could not be avoided. However, it also proved that the partisan movement was indestructible. In later operations, especially during the Fourth and other enemy offensives, the enemy forces were continuously reinforced. Of course, the strengthening of enemy's army spelled heavy losses for the people's liberation army. But it was just through such strife with the enemy that the People's Liberation Movement developed into a true national army.

6

The people's liberation movement in the Bosanska Krajina had to struggle on several fronts. Along with the merciless war against the invader, the movement also had to fight against the fratricidal policy of the ustaše movement and state aimed at disuniting the Serbs, Croats and Moslems. It had to de-mystify četnik slogans and fight against the illusions sown by the četniks among the Serbian part of the population. Through this double political struggle, the movement gained the overall support of Serbian, Croatian and Moslem people, as the only fighter for their interests, for their common life on the same land. The ranks of the movement were wide open to everyone who wanted to fight the invader. In spite of the ravage and destruction wrought by the war, everybody could feel deeply the vision of common future life on the freed territories, won and fought for by the Krajina units, from the first guerilla detachments to large partisan battalions, brigades, divisions and corps. The stability and the finality of this territory were further enhanced by the fact that most of the Krajina townlets were on the liberated territory for a longer time than under occupation; besides, in the early years of war, the towns of Bihać, Jajce, Mrkonjić-Grad and Sanski Most were centres in which historical state decisions were made, both for Yugoslavia and for Bosnia and Herzegovina. It was no chance that this territory was called spontaneously the "Bihać republic" at the time when the elite proletarian units — central units of the People's Liberation Movement in Yugoslavia — were already on the territory, and when the first contours of the new Yugoslav state were drawn up at the first session of the AVNOJ (Antifascist Council of the People's Liberation of Yugoslavia) in liberated Bihać in November, 1942.

The decision of the Supreme Staff of the People's Liberation Army on the creation of the people's liberation army of Yugoslavia was also made in the proper place (Bosanski Petrovac), for the Bosanska Krajina — along with all victims of the war — also gave this army 22 shock brigades which fought all over Yugoslavia. Thence the still visionary sound of the recognition of Krajina's merits, voiced by comrade Tito in Srpska Jasenica on January 7, 1943 when reviewing the Fourth Krajina Shock Brigade: "You are the pillar and the foundation of our people's liberation army in this fateful hour ... Be proud of being in the first ranks of the fight for freedom both in the army and in the background". With particular passion, the Krajina brigades tried on several occasions to free Banjaluka. Finally, they succeeded, on April 22, 1945, in liberating this town, which was always the focus of revolutionary movements in the Bosanska Krajina, which gave all its revolutionary human resources to its country in the fateful hours, and which issued the first order to start armed resistance in the Bosanska Krajina.

STOJANKA, MOTHER OF KNEŽPOLJE
(fragment)

. . . Oh! my three wolves and three bitter snowstorms,
let your mother kiss you icy.
Roll up your sleeve, Srđan,
your mother will know you easily:
a mole on your left arm: a dark blackberry!
Roll up, son Mrđan,
roll up your right leg:
this is where the first bullet
pierced your shin!
And you, Mlađen, laugh dead to your mother,
she would know you best:
the four eye-teeth
that outgrew the others
like in a he-wolf!

Woe, my three birthmarks,
woe, my three irate vipers from the sunny slope,
sucked by your mother with valiant force,
engraved with a bullet's trace by the revolt,
Woe,
where are you?
Are you bemoaned
by the waters of the Mlječanica,
or of the Gračanica,
or of the Moštanica,
or are you eaten away
by the yellow worms
in the beastly black trenches,
on the beastly many-toothed wire,
along the Dubica road?

Stand up, rise,
look down the Knežpolje plain!
Is that the Knežpolje of yesterday?
Is this, children, before autumn?
Where are the white and bent reapers?
Under which ripening pear-tree
there awaits
the friendly and sunburnt reapers
a large flushed pie
of true free wheat
and a large bowl of sour milk?

And from the Kozara, my own, all the way to the Sava,
the crops burst, from freedom,
as from water,
the maize is like a green army,
the pregnant wheat totters,
the plums have blued the trees,
with their sweet burden,
sprawling them, with their weight,
like cows with young.
There is bread, honey and fruit everywhere,
over head and ears,
the earth is brimming as a heaped beehive,
waiting, my own, for the sweat,
of brawny male muscles . . .

But waiting in vain, in vain!

                    Skender KULENOVIĆ

Refugees

Together with the peoples of Yugoslavia, the people of Bosnia and Herzegovina gave great sacrifices in the liberation war, in the fight against the invaders and national traitors. The sacrifices of the people of this region, of the Bosanska Krajina, were particularly heavy. In this fight they did not regret their human and material losses, they gave everything they could, deeply aware that without those sacrifices present-day socialist Yugoslavia would not have become a reality.

It is a fact that there is no mother, in this region, that did not send a son or daughter into the fight, and no family that did not lose somebody in it.

Đuro Pucar

The pioneers' company

Performance of the People's Liberation Theatre, Podgrmeč, 1942

The Fifth Krajina Brigade crosses the Vrbanja, May 1943

The partisan hospital

The army and the people were one

The Kozara »kolo«

Units of the 10th Division entering Banjaluka on April 22, 1945

Banjaluka, destroyed and ravaged by the war, was reconstructed after the Liberation, from 1945 to 1947. The socialist system provided the incentive for the vigorous development of industry and social activities. Five years after the end of the war, Banjaluka had 36 enterprises, the most important being: the Rudi Čajavec Electronics and Electromechanics Factory, the Jelšingrad Machine Works and Steel Foundry, the Krajina Building Construction Enterprise, the Vrbas Wood and Timber Industry, the Vitaminka Fruit Juice and Canning Factory, the Bosna Footwear Factory, the Elektro-Banjaluka Enterprise for the Production and Distribution of Electric Power, the Autoprevoz Transportation Enterprise, and several service enterprise: Instalater, 29. Novembar, Elmont, Autokrajina, Autoservis, the Projekt Design Office, and others.

The period from 1951 to 1955 was marked by the implementation of the Law on Workers' Self-government in the Economy, by the formation of workers' councils and management boards in enterprises. For the first time in the history of human society, the workers' class of Yugoslavia became the subject of the process of production and income distribution. The working ability and the initiative of all citizens gained greater significance. The enterprises of Banjaluka increased their manufacturing facilities, modernized and rationalized their business operations. Several new enterprises were also founded. The largest enterprise built in this period was the Cellulose Factory.

Seven new enterprises were formed in the period between 1956 and 1960, the most important having been the Kosmos Enterprise, the Service Enterprise 1. Maj, the Univerzal Hydraulic Equipment Works, and the Lasta Transportation Agency.

The economic strengthening of Banjaluka continued from 1961 to 1969. The Cellulose Factory added, to its already existing plants, a plant for the production of viscose, paper and ready-made paper products. The Vrbas Wood and Timber Enterprise built a new furniture factory. Through the construction of new plants, and revamping of existing capital equipment, all the town's enterprises constantly expanded the material basis of their business operations. The tourist trade and commerce developed too. The conditions for the advancement of these activities were extremely favourable. In terms of its geographic and economic position, Banjaluka is at the centre of the main arteries, and goods and tourist flows, in the north—south and east—west direction. In the most recent years, the economy of Banjaluka undertook major steps forward, and concentrated its resources through merger with other similar enterprises in the town and other parts of Yugoslavia.

Such a dynamic development of the town over the quarter-century of its life and work in socialist society has brought about positive qualitative and quantitative changes in all areas of life. The economy and industry grew several times as compared to what had been built in Banjaluka up to 1945. The new modern and large industrial plants and modern technology (electronics, electromechanics, chemistry) gave a new qualitative feature to the economy of Banjaluka. However, the balanced economic growth did not involve the entire area of the Banjaluka commune, and the vaster area of the Bosanska Krajina region, which remained economically underdeveloped, with a low national income (4,700 dinars per capita in the Banjaluka commune). This had a retarding effect on the growth of the town, which could have developed more rapidly had its vaster area of gravitation — the Bosanska Krajina — developed more optimally over the past period.

The attained level of economic development is best seen in the dominant share of industry in the creation of social product — 46.8%, higher than that of any other branch of the economy. Through exports of their products, the manufacturers of Banjaluka have gained recognition and strengthened their positions in the markets of numerous foreign countries.

The substantial economic growth of the town has been followed by adequate changes in the field of welfare and standard of living. The population of the town increased from 32,000 in 1939 to 75,000 in 1969. Today Banjaluka has 76 enterprises; in 1939 there were 4 enterprises, four workshops, and a number of shops. The economy of the town employed 5,000 people in 1939; in September, 1969, the number of employed persons amounted to 30,730. In 1939 the households of the town used 390,000 kWh of electric power; in 1969, the figure was 38 million kWh. Several new housing units have also been built in the post-war period: Čaire, Mejdan I, Mejdan II, Rosulje and Hiseta. Altogether more than 11,000 new flats have been built. The new traffic arteries got an asphalt cover; most of the town districts and streets have been provided with the necessary utilities. New tree promenades, parks, lawns and gardens have been planted. Banjaluka has remained a town of lush greenery.

The health service has undergone intensive development. Private medical service is no longer sought so much. Health centres, medical care centres with specialist services, and outpatient care departments in enterprises are being developed. The General Hospital with specialist wards and laboratories, the Children's Hospital, the Hospital for Skin and Mycotic Diseases, the Health Centre with general and specialist outpatpatient departments and First Aid Station, the Institute for Health Protection with the epidemiological, bacteriological and labour medicine department and appropriate laboratories, the pharmaceutical service and health centre of the Cellulose Factory (merged into the Medical Centre in 1957), the Institute for Medical Rehabilitation and the independent health stations of the railway employees, of the Electronic Industry, and of the Vrbas Enterprise, with altogether 1,560 beds (as compared to 210 in 1940) and 129 doctors (as compared to 8 in 1940), provide medical care for one million five hundred thousand inhabitants.

By the number and structure of schools Banjaluka may be classed among the towns with a well-developed school network. One out of four citizens of the Banjaluka commune is a school pupil or student. Before the earthquake, the 14 urban and 63 rural primary schools were attended by 26,322 pupils, and the 12 secondary schools by 8,768 pupils; the three schools of higher learning and the Faculty of Engineering had 2,500 students, i. e. altogether 37,590 pupils and students. Teaching was taken care of by 1350 teachers and professors.

...and they were... and they were —
ten to one...

Those were the hard, but glorious days during which our people showed that no sacrifices were too difficult for them when freedom and survival are involved.

(from a letter of Marshal Tito to the veterans of Bosanska Krajina).

Šoša Mažar among the fighters of the Banjaluka company

Young fighters of the Banjaluka partisan company

Jovan Bijelić (1886—1964), the Red Mist. Poet of the spectral visions of native motifs, Bijelić fills his works with the general human restlessness and elementary nature of the native soil. His landscape painting is defined by the colours of the morning sun and dusk, by the red-hot streams of love, by faith and brave distress. The area of the picture is relieved of details. Bijelić's spontaneous and defiant serenity unites poetry and wisdom, and gives a creative meaning to the incomprehensible. This joy and truth is borne to the peak in its full light, through troubled and terrifying silence, tragic thunder, and large and heavy clouds full of reflexes. The Bosnian landscape has become man's authentic discovery, the landscape of the painter's soul, where the objects are on an equal footing with the incessant and victorious struggle of the spirit.

SONG OF THE DEAD PROLETARIANS

...And on the thirteenth, dark and rainy night, several
squads of Krajina proletarians, surrounded round the hospital in the mountain, made their last charge against a ten
times stronger enemy, and fell bravely in the unequal fight...

(according to a report)

In our country wheat is shooting out into ears, sown by our hands,
harvest awaits us, and the girls' song:
at dusk, melancholy and soft,
and we have fallen, comrade,
fallen is the wheat, young, green, the early spring harvest,
misty sorrows, and the whisper of rain, circle over the dead song

Dead are the hands and the rifles,
formed in death,
comrade next to comrade;
and they were... and they were —
ten to one.

Ten to one in a rainy night, and we were tired,
hungry and wet, ten beasts to one.
One to ten, one to ten! Oh, is that possible?
Yes, — we are proletarians!

When we left home, many a tear bid us farewell
and the native mounts murmured thoughtfully:
Oh, will they ever come back?
The old mothers are waiting, and the sleepless nights trickling,
and the eye keeps guard down the road:
to await a messenger from us.

New youth will come, to bring new days
and continue our songs unsung,
forged in live fire. —
Oh, we have started these songs, through them we speak from afar,
reminding the sister of a brother, the girl of a sweetheart,
and the sad mother of a son.

And the day of glory will come, victory will be ours,
the wild beasts will disappear,
and Freedom's troops will march,
with the dead proletarians.

Branko ĆOPIĆ

Krajina partisans on the march

Ten Krajina brigades were formed in 1942

Withdrawal of wounded fighters

Immediately after the liberation of the town and of the country the educational policy was subordinated to the idea of eradicating the inherited backwardness and developing a system of socialist education and schooling. Such aspirations allowed for major expansion of schooling, although the necessary prerequisites still lacked. This required the opening of new schools, two- and four-grade high schools, secondary vocational schools, which were later on followed by the Higher School of Pedagogy, the Higher School of Agriculture, the Higher School of Economics and the Faculty of Engineering. Thus Banjaluka became an educational centre, not only for its own limited area, but also for the entire region of Bosanska Krajina.

The schooling reform provided a new impulse to the development of the educational system, it brought school closer to life, introduced new teaching techniques, democratic educational methods, and permitted man's overall growth. Self-government was also introduced in schools. Major progress in the construction of school buildings was made in 1966, when the citizens decided in favour of a voluntary contribution for the building of schools. The appearance of young painters and art educators meant the recognition of modern art and modern art education. The drawings of the children from the primary schools of Banjaluka have been particularly noted on Yugoslav and international exhibitions, and have always won general recognition and high ratings.

In the post-war years the cultural endeavours went hand in hand with the development of the town. The National Theatre renewed its activities and adjusted its repertoire to the new requirements of drama art and theatre audiences; the Ethnographic Museum obtained new collections and additional space, and it became the Museum of the Bosanska Krajina Region; among the other promoters of the town's cultural life, particular mention should be made of the Petar Kočić National Library, the Archives of the Bosanska Krajina Region, the Banjaluka Broadcasting Station, the cultural societies Pelagić, Veselin Masleša and KAB; the Children's Theatre was also founded. Cultural activities had a marked progress among the youth. From their ranks there grew a number of gifted artists who would later on gain renown in the major cultural centres of the country. The Culture Hall organizes concerts with appearances of the most eminent Yugoslav and foreign artists, numerous painting exhibitions, lectures, and literary evenings.

Printed for the first time on the liberated territory of the Bosanska Krajina during the People's Liberation War, the newspaper Glas (The Voice) has regularly been printed after the war as a weekly. Other periodical publications are also being printed (poem collections, writings on Banjaluka's past and local folklore, the papers of the Bosanska Krajina Museum, writings on the People's Liberation War in the Krajina region). The youth paper Mladi Krajišnik (The Young Man of Krajina) has been edited with great success for several years. In 1955 a group of young writers started the journal Korijen (Root). In 1960 another review was started — Putevi (Paths); its contributors were numergus young poets, storytellers, literary, art and music critics, from all over Yugoslavia, and especially from Banjaluka and Bosnia. Particular attention is devoted to the cultural heritage, both Yugoslav and regional, keeping concurrently the pace with modern trends. Other important publications comprise the journal for language and literature teaching Prilozi (Contributions), the medical review Scripta Medica, and — since very recently — the Journal of the National Theatre.

The richness and expressiveness of the new trends in the art creativity of Banjaluka attract special attention. Banjaluka has had a considerable painting tradition. Already before World War One Austrian and Czech painters used to come to Banjaluka, trying to approach the exotic folklore motifs and to gain inspiration therein; among the students of the Banjaluka High School there were, at the time, the later well-known Yugoslav painters M. Uzelac and V. Gecan. In the period between the two wars, Špiro Bocarić, one of the leading Bosnian painters, spent the last years of his life in Banjaluka. Up to 1932 one of the town's citizens was also the gifted impressionist painter Pero Popović (1881—1941), whose paintings express "through their vivid drawing and daring contrasts of coloristic and light relationships" the typical local impetuosity, misgiving and fleeting penetration.

The link between pre-war and post-war painting in Banjaluka was provided by Božo Nikolić (1904—1958), from Banjaluka itself, whose painter's profile had already been established between the two wars, especially in water--colours. After the liberation he continued painting Bosanska Krajina landscapes and everyday life scenes. Since 1956, Banjaluka has given quite a few young painters of powerful artistic vocation and lucidity, who already attract the attention of the wider Yugoslav public. Some of them have also already been noted at exhibitions abroad.

Thanks to the progress in the field of sports activities, the sportsmen of Banjaluka have been taking part in the top Yugoslav competitions. The hand--ball players of the Borac Club were Yugoslav champions in 1958—1959 and 1959—1960, and Yugoslav Cup winners in 1957, 1958, 1960 and 1969. The Borac football team competed in the First Federal League in 1961, and has again joined the league this year. The success of the chess players, basket ball players, boxers, field and track athletes, gymnasts, kayak-rowers, parachutists and cyclists, marksmen and motorbike racers, proves that Banjaluka has become an important sports centre. Quite a few Banjaluka sportsmen, men and women alike, have worn the dress of the Yugoslav national team.

The natural position of Banjaluka, its cultural riches, historic past and overall development have increasingly aroused general attention, and it has also become an important tourist attraction. Its attractions include the clear green river with its islands and nice natural beaches, picturesque canyons and old water-mills, the surounding hills with orchards, glades, woods and game reserves, sources of warm mineral water, the picturesque roads, and the numerous tourist and excursion resorts. According to an old writing, any friendly traveller who passes through this town will remember it forever, and wish to come back to it. Today, as years go by, the impulse for such an experience becomes stronger and more evident.

Welcome, liberators!

Tito in Banjaluka (1945).

Meeting of the Krajina brigades

Veterans' mothers.

Construction of the Doboj — Banjaluka railway.

Respond, oh restless river,
stuck into my heart like a flower;
I waited for you all night on the bank,
while you lay before me — uncaught.

You spurt from two green breasts
and flow along my outstretched fingers;
I pick your water curls with my eyes,
while the hungry rays of morning browse them.

From your depths, as from a riddle,
in a fleeting moment the limestone splashes,
on which water writes out its lines,
as the eyes write out love on desired thighs.

Ismet BEKRIĆ

SHEPHERDESS

The shepherdess offers me
Red strawberries
Cooled in the mountain snow
Eyes
Blue hues of the mounts
The landscape has stopped to rest
At noon.

Dušan MUTIĆ

WITNESS OF ONE'S OWN STEADINESS

Man's time
Of man
Leaves
A trace of knowledge
To which you pray
Washing you eyes
With its water
And confirm yourself
With your pace.

Mesud ISLAMOVIĆ

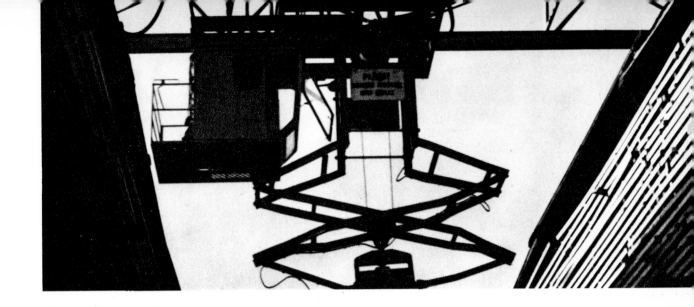

In the Jelšingrad Foundry

A plant of the Bosna Footwear Factory

The future metal workers

In the fields of the Mladen Stojanović Farming Estate

The town bridge

Cellulose and Paper Factory

THE KRAJINA CARYATID

Before her I put down my verse
about that what it gives me
and tells me silently
murmuring through its hues
and foreboding through its colours.

Grown together with forehead's line
grown into shoulder's mountain
leaden and with the roses
of the sun and snowflakes
pebbles and blades
the vaults of the small land
to which by destiny
it rose by its birth
from the mountainous depths
from the roots of dark blackberries
from the ferns
and from the stubble-fields
where crickets and grasshoppers
travel and mourn

Dug into the soil like a tree
built high into the vault
embroidered like a garden
all the treasure of poverty
it grasped softly in its bosom
embraced it raptly with its arms
and it breathes from the depths
as the soul of the small land
bestowing a wedding present to everyone
while saying its silent song.

Nasiha Kapidžić-Hadžić

SPRING SONG

The snows are disappearing and the fragrant myrtle is felt by the distant waters. The windows are full of bulls and wild brooks. My jug is becoming golden and the sun is large. Now the spider has sunk too into the crystal tower. His home is a bulwark of light.

Everything is blue, and blood is shed in the evening west. I know: I will again light the candle, watch my shadow flickering on the walls, and then dream — for a long time — of when it will finally move into the spider's castle. Only here one may think — without fear — of the wind that bemoaned me last winter.

A butterfly flies into the room and I close the windows quickly. I say: rest next to the flame, my candle will not kill you.

Nenad RADANOVIĆ

Laboratory of the Faculty of Engineering

A plant of the Electronic Industry

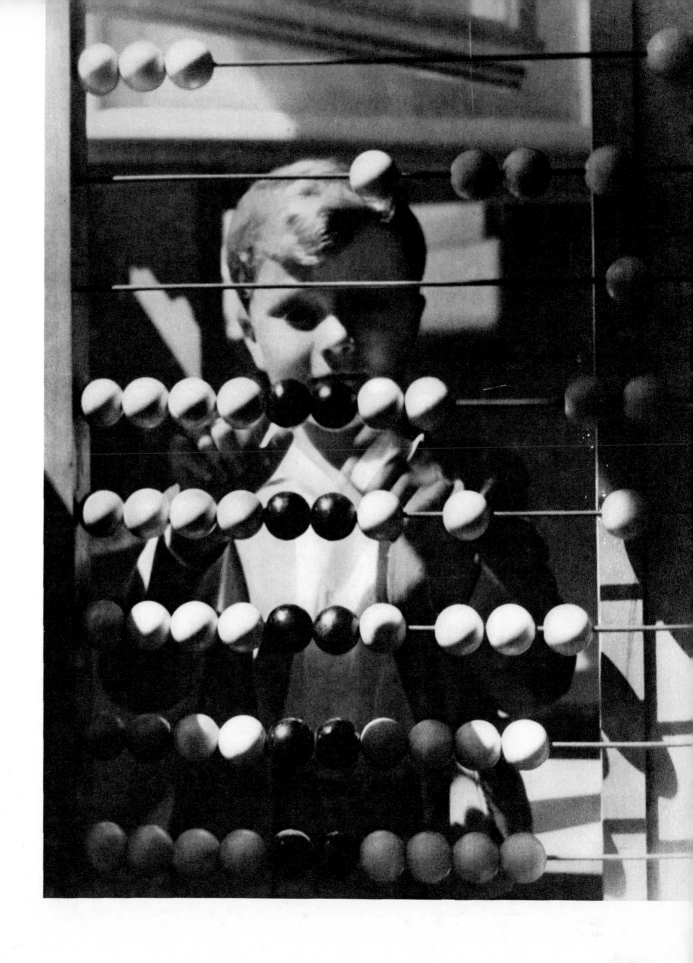

National Theatre of the Bosanska Krajina — stage

Culture Hall

Božo
Nikolić
(1904—1958),
Still Life
Distemper

Tomislav Dugonjić, Composition — graphic drawing

The Ferhadija Mosque, endowment of Ferhad-Pasha Sokolović; built in 1579. Its ground plan, high minaret, harmonious lines and elegant inner arrangement and decorations, make it one of the most beautiful monuments of Islamic culture in Bosnia and Herzegovina.

Banjaluka is the transition from east to west, but it is nevertheless a true Bosnian town.

Were there no tree promenades and parks, the towns would forget the birds' twitter.

Meeting
of the old
and the new

Stadium of the Borac football club

MINARET

The rock begot you,
placed you into a cloud
and bestowed the mark of eternity.
Centuries tread past you,
and lightning
makes you a jewel.

Demonic spite
gives you beauty.
At times
you plunge into mist
and start
then,
a raven hawk hounded to you.

You have been born a long time ago,
man,
a long time ago.
When the rock begets you again,
you shall become a minaret.

Jovan BOJOVIĆ

EPITAPH TO THE LIVING

dead and nicely forgotten you are in your body
and you walk laugh breathe envenom love
everthing bound to you and close to you
through shackles you see suffer live

you do not walk the earth but a variant of death
you do not breathe air but the words of a new song
you love but the conception of evil
and that with what you deceive yourself
is not life but nothingness inherited with birth

alive you are and nicely deceived in our tomb
by air flowers sunshine snakes and human flesh:
ALIVE YOU ARE AND PITIED THEREFORE!

Ranko PRERADOVIĆ

Tijesno — the Vrbas canyon

On Sunday, October 26, 1969, at 06.37.11 p.m., the town of Banjaluka and the surrounding region of 11,000 square kilometres, with almost 800,000 inhabitants, was shaken by an earthquake the strength of which was up to 8 degrees of the Mercalli scale. The earth trembled. Chimneys, power pylons and house gables tumbled down. Anxiety and fear held the town. People ran into the streets — alarmed and helpless. After 6 minutes and 10 seconds, there was another earthquake. Its force — more than five degrees.

Immediately after the second shock the members of the Civil Defense Staff and political workers met in the Town Hall. The first measures were undertaken: data were collected regarding the situation in the field; civil defense teams from various enterprises moved into action. Units of the Banjaluka garrison were already in the streets — assisting the imperilled population. The number of policemen in the streets was increased, and so was the number of traffic policemen on the crossroads.

The hospital buildings were heavily damaged. The soldiers and medical staff transferred the patients into the yard and basement. Medical teams offered first aid to the injured persons in the streets. The Banjaluka garrison, the Red Cross and the Welfare Centre made their reserves available — tents and blankets. All aid was sent to the Medical Centre where it was needed the most. More and more people arrived to their enterprises to clear up the ruins and save the machines.

The self-organization of the citizens and the numerous spontaneous actions were the logical consequence of the twenty-year self-government experience. The organizations of the League of Communists, of the Socialist Alliance of the Working People, and the trade unions and youth, aldermen, federal and republican deputies — all found soon their bearings and joined action. In the Town Hall, local communities, and in enterprises extensive measures were undertaken to accommodate the population. Yugoslav Army soldiers were available at every point in the town. The military commanders acted hand in hand with the Civil Defense Staff and socio-political organizations. During the night the Banjaluka Broadcasting Station broadcasted the decision of the Civil Defense Staff — until expert examination of the buildings all public meetings indoors were prohibited; shops were to remain closed; teaching in schools would be interrupted.

The night was long and cold. Thousands of fires, and chilled and tired people round them, could be seen everywhere: in the streets, parks and gardens, graveyards and village clearings, on the banks of the Vrbas and on sports grounds. The earth never stopped trembling. One hundred and sixty engineers and technicians, divided into teams, checked the buildings and established the degree of damage.

Morning, October 27. An extensive report, regarding the situation in the field and actions under way, was submitted at the meeting of local and republican officials (who had arrived to Banjaluka during the night). The indispensable measures for the following days were also laid down.

At 09.11.33 a. m. the earth shook again. This time the earthquake was stronger than the first one. The impact attained nine degrees of the Mercalli scale. Somewhere, deep in the earth, under people's feet, released energy thundered. Buildings jarred, and walls tottered. Roofs and cupolas crashed into the streets. The town collapsed. In the streets — fear, thousands of frightened people. Motor-car horns wailed. The dust obscured the sun.

After a moment of passing confusion, common sense and self-confidence prevailed again. Soldiers, youth, citizens drew the dead and wounded out of the ruins. Injured people arrived from all parts to the courtyard of the demolished hospital — on carts, stretchers, in the arms of their neighbours, by themselves. Transfusions and complicated surgical interventions were carried out on the lawn and in the hospital park. The maternity ward — in the tents. The large Titanik housing block, the High School building, the Nurse School building, the building of the Institute for Medical Rehabilitation, military buildings, and thousands of other buildings were completely destroyed. The sub--stations were demolished, and the lines broken. There were no telephone connections. Amateur radio operators broadcast their sad message: Banjaluka lies in ruins.

Major casualties were avoided thanks to the precautions taken immediately after the first shock. However, the balance was tragic — 15 dead and 1,250 wounded.

Tanks and bulldozers cleared the streets for traffic. News of destruction and damage began to arrive from the Krajina communes. Throughout the day Yugoslav and foreign stations broadcast calls for help. News agencies and special newspaper editions kept publishing news on the disaster in the Krajina. Air force, civil and police aircraft landed on the Zalužani airport, bringing blood plasma and drugs, and taking away the most severely injured. Columns of trucks from all parts of Yugoslavia, from all republics, and neighbouring countries, already sped to Banjaluka, bringing food, blankets, tents; teams of doctors, seismologists, statics experts, civil engineers kept arriving... The approaches to the town were jammed.

The affected area was faced with inconceivable consequences. There were no flats. Any economic activity was impossible. School buildings and research laboratories were destroyed, and so were the modern hospital facilities. In one fleeting moment everything had been lost.

The situation required fast, comprehensive and synchronized measures, both of momentary and long-term scope, in all areas of social life, in order to provide for more bearable living and working conditions in the affected area, and for the activity of social organizations. Epidemiological measures were undertaken in order to prevent the appearance of infectious diseases. Major efforts were invested into the capacitation of the power, water supply and sewage network. Due care was paid to the protection of social and private property. There were no violations or thefts. Everything was done to start — at least partly — production, open the shops and restaurants. Salaries, pensions, scholarships and welfare checks were paid out normally. Shops were improvised in the streets. No later than three days after the earthquake the region began to lead a more normal economic life. Damaged roofs were repaired; buildings that could stand, at least for a time, were supported. Experts elaborated programmes of seismologic and geoseismic exploration, the town planners established the first permanent locations of the new settlements; enterprises drew up reconstruction studies with programmes of long-term development with the assistance of numerous institutions and international organizations; the Direction for Banjaluka's reconstruction was established. Everywhere the battle for tomorrow was fought. Tito's visit to destroyed Banjaluka encouraged the people, gave them new strength to withstand the hardships and overcome them, with the assistance of all the peoples of Yugoslavia.

Krajina resisted stoically. People carried the pain in themselves, but subdued it. 46,000 inhabitants lived in tents. 15,000 families were accommodated in partly repaired buildings, trailers, garages, railway waggons, sheds, huts, in newly built flats, basements, and less damaged buildings of their neighbours. 205 railway waggons, 2,700 trailers and 170 sheds were prepared for provisional quarters. The long winter months were ahead.

And when one believed that the danger had passed, when the people of Banjaluka tried to celebrate the New Year and forget, for a moment, their hardships, another earthquake — the 258th — of 6.5 degree force, shook the confidence that the ground was calming down, aroused new doubts and created new thousands of homeless people. Some still usable buildings, and partly repaired ones, were damaged and became too dangerous for use.

The disaster, pain and destruction which beset Banjaluka through the terrifying earthquake determined — suddenly and mercilessly — the new decisive hour of its history.

The army was with the people. The tank drivers, infantry, the sanitary and supply services, and the engineers cleared the streets and assisted the jeoparized population. Units from other garrisons joined them. An army field hospital was made available, with a complete surgery team, blood plasma, and a considerable supply of drugs and medical materials. The army provided tents for more than 20,000 people, prepared warm meals and bread, helped in the repair of the city water supply system, supplied the citizens with water by means of its tank cars, took part in the organization of life in the local communities. The army worked hard for five days on end. After the first assistance, the work was continued by the sappers, who demolished — during the autumn and winter — the heavily damaged buildings marked with yellow signs. The units of the Banjaluka garrison remained in the town, in their destroyed barracks: they repaired them, went on with military training. In winter and spring, they were in the streets again, helping the population to overcome the snow drifts and floods.

In the hardest moments of destruction, the health service was both fast and well organized. Medical teams assisted the injured among the ruins, on the lawns, and in the hospital yards. The earthquake destroyed the buildings of the Surgery Ward with otolaryngology, the Obstetrics and Maternity Ward, the neuropsychiatric ward, the X-ray and interne medicine ward, the lung disease ward. The hospital for skin and venereal diseases, the Institute for medical rehabilitation, and many health centres did not withstand the impact either ... The wounded and the grave patients were evacuated within the first few hours by helicopter, bus, and ambulance. In the provisional settlements and camps, enterprises and villages, in tents, waggons and trailers, sheds and less damaged schools, the medical staff took care of the children and old people, of their ill and exhausted fellow-citizens. No effort was spared in order to prevent the appearance of infectious diseases. There were no working hours or duty turns — one worked without stopping.

The situation was also very grave and complex in the field of education. More than 60 school buildings were destroyed or damaged in the urban area, and 37,000 pupils and students remained without hostels and schools. From November 11 to December 1, 1969, Banjaluka evacuated 10,000 pupils and teachers, i. e. 17 primary and secondary schools. That was another shock for the children and their parents, and for the whole town.

The schools were transferred everywhere; some of them were even moved to different republics. The evacuated school collectives met with quite a few problems. The hotel buildings in which the schools were, generally, accommodated were not equipped for winter living and school work. Teaching aids and libraries were scarce. All this required a lot of ingenuity and self-denial.

The hosts did everything in their power to help their guests overcome the numerous difficulties. For the teachers, that was a major commitment and responsibility. The teachers replaced the children's parents.

The children who had remained in the ruined town fared even worse. Railway waggons and buses were turned into classrooms. Sheds were built, some damaged schools repaired, as well as some social halls. However, only in January did the first school bell mark the beginning of teaching.

Before the beginning of the tourist season, the evacuated schools had to end their programmes. From April 22 to 26, 1970, the children of Banjaluka kept coming home. The ruined town met them joyfully and warmly.

The cultural heritage of the town was also mutilated. Cracks appeared on the walls of the Ferhadija Mosque, outstanding monument of Moslem architecture in Bosnia; its slender minaret crumbled down. The white stone of the Arnaudija Mosque is broken by dark lines which impair its harmony. The Franciscan monastery and the Petrićevac church no longer exist — their walls, high vaults and belfry staircases did not withstand the destructive seconds of shock. The earthquake destroyed the sculptures, frescoes and carvings in the trappist church of Delibašino Selo. The ancient Kastel fortress, with the buildings of the Bosanska Krajina Museum, lies in ruins. The shock also damaged the Watch-Tower, the Gomionica monastery, and other buildings of a cultural nature: the National Library, the Culture Hall, the Art Gallery, the Bosanska Krajina Archives... The curtain of the National Theatre descended at the very moment of its fortieth anniversary. The building of the Children's Theatre was also heavily damaged, which deprived the children of their favourite puppet heroes.

And yet, in the sight of the inner eye, in the lucid thought which remembers and knows, the traces of the creative spiritual aspirations on this soil, in this world, are the powerful pulse of life which goes on. Many artists have already tried to transpose the drama of Banjaluka into a durable symbol of testimony. Among the important endeavours in the field of spiritual creativity one may list the soul-stirring film and TV presentations of the earthquake, the symphony Banjaluka 69, composed by the Banjaluka composer and connoisseur of Krajina folklore Vlado Milošević in the days immediately after the earthquake, the numerous poems which have already been published, the review called Tomorrow by the young full of optimism. All these pictures, in which the images of reality and the signs of the vital mental condition are clearly seen, have successfully drawn and presented the moments of Krajina's defiance and silence after the October of 1969.

Oh, wounded town,
who broke your wings?
I had you on my palm,
in my eye,
in my heart,
and now your fragile fragments,
pierce my pupils

The terrifying moment when a town disappears before people's eyes, and when houses are turned into broken bricks and pillars.

That morning, after a sleepless night, full of wounds, ill omens, sorrow and hate for the elements that destroyed you and that cannot be grasped, the town staggered, trembled and rose in pain and mute moan. Roofs flew, walls broke and disappeared. Houses crumbled down. Clouds of swirling dust and smoke rose to the sky; thunder gave in to gloom and ominous silence, which rang in our ears as the hammer of fate. And the town had a great heart, and its people remained on their feet.

Vilko Vinterhalter

Banjaluka wrapped in woe and sorrow.

Tito in the destroyed Medical Centre

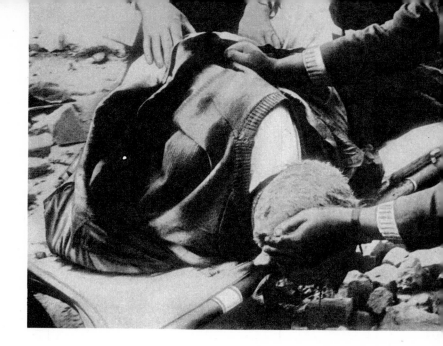

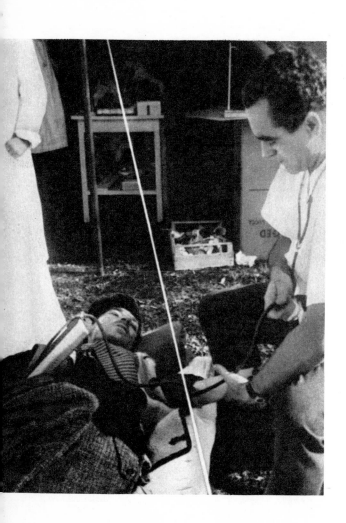

The sombre statistical data are recorded

View of the town and the park

Panorama grada i park

MORNING OF NOVEMBER 1, 1969

In the town of Banja Luka, hell's playground... The altars are destroyed. Morning has remained. Once again it thaws anxiety in the bosom. Everybody flees to the arms of the garden. A man is being pulled out of a room as a healthy tooth out of the jaw. A house is being torn from the heart. Vain lie the chimneys among flowers. Roofs flee the smoke, and stoves the fire. Fire escapes men. A mute dance of warm words round the hearth. From panic, from the sky, fish have returned drowned by dust. Meanwhile — among the chaos of pain and suffering — earth has eluded the frightened steps. And the mainstream of the river has escaped the fish.

Children-less, the houses hang like slaughtered sheep. Bursting violins swim in the "Renaissance" workshop of master Ljubović. Bricks have scattered guitars' frenzied wires. Let them ruminate, as a memento of the elements. Romeo's bicycle has been shattered by Juliet's fallen balcony. Silver, morning, gold — an impossible song knocks on the gates of the paper mill. It offers blood to the paper... Hills afford no escape, either to devil or man. They say that in the land of poetry white wings are woven for the boats on the river. Marble lies in the graveyard, pecking irony. There is no return. The Vrbas cannot be tied into a loop, nor will it be conquered by bewilderment. Life hurries to meet itself. Gipsy children are crying in their motley rags, driving away the mist and hanging on their mothers' necks. Leaves cannot be counted but with the nose, with the smell of the rotten and fallen. The town's canyons are terrified, and the parks gape emptily. The wooden bridge moans under the burden of the sun. In the air, in space, worries have escaped the wanderers' tents to cough up their frosty breath. Fortresses tremble before the horsemen that will bring fate to the well. Angels pull the thirsty chariots. Carts full of empty gourds to help the clumsy swimmers through infernal feasts, despoiled of serenity and peace. The heavenly scorn, as usually, now falls freely in its star dust over the treasures of the town earned with bloody toil.

"...and their gardens were like paradise..." The icy and pale lip of the moon is mysteriously silent above our heads, as if opening the vessel of winter. Old people say that we often used to look at gipsies with an evil eye... dirtying a crust of bread. The claw of the wind from below amuses Satan, tearing away clock's hands. In the bed of the dry river of the main street, a painter died, for he was thought a hyena, a machine for turning grief into money. We have also found out that even the hooligan Fufto shed a tear for the old school which he fled like a dragon. Even he, whose one ear crows entered to come out as a flight of warblers. For three hundred and ninety years beggars upside down. Everything but man's arms, shorter for a minaret, longer for a spite. In the town-defiance, hell's playground. In Banja Luka, herbarium of hvae been asking for alms in front of the mosque. Now, everything is lame and serenades.

Alojz ĆURIĆ

DEVIL'S MESSIAH

Oppressed by the mountains,
under the ridges,
tied by the hardest bonds
beyond reason, beneath the world
in the dark regions
of depths and chasms.
Thus strained
he is quiet as a birch-tree
in the sunny morning,
quieter than the linden
when the wind sleeps.
From his voice
a snake shoots out.
For he need only wink,
and the earth will tremble
as a live heart on a knife's tip,
how many vipers open suddenly,
how many souls flee the mouth,
the lightning becomes tame and silent in fright,
what is thunder to his breath,
as sparks from pure girls' hair.
And yet he, the architect
builds lighthouses
on his shoulder,
on flame,
he re-builds the destroyed Skadars,
and Banja Lukas,
and triumphal arches,
for the devil's might crushes everything
but not him.

          Nikola TOMOVIĆ

Work and agreement

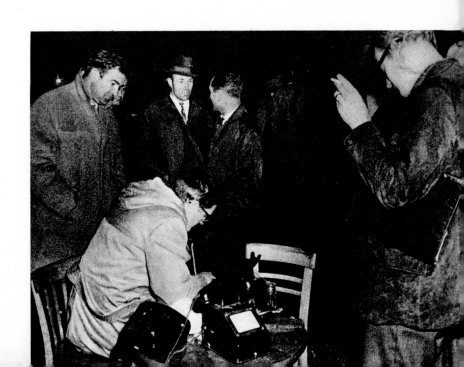

People were left homeless

Industry suffered major losses

I never heard the order, perhaps it was even given, I have never seen warriors during a charge, but I saw these young fellows rushing up the hill of mortar and concrete blocks, easily and freely as one rushes on a flat field.

Now only the willingness is left,
our strength for this town of ours

Dwellers of the abandoned track

The entire organization of society, the staffs, the representative and self-government bodies, the political and other organizations functioned well from the beginning. The solidarity of all our peoples and nationalities was efficient and unselfish. On the very first day, help arrived from all over Yugoslavia — Zagreb, Belgrade, Sarajevo, Skopje, Titograd, Ljubljana, Priština, Novi Sad, and other towns.

Branko Mikulić

Towns are not buildings only, but people

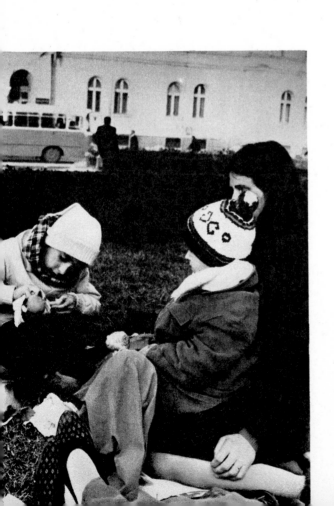

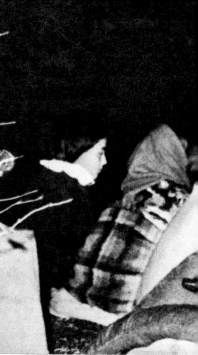
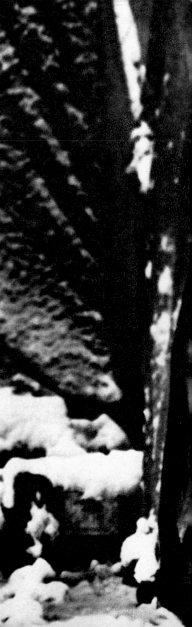

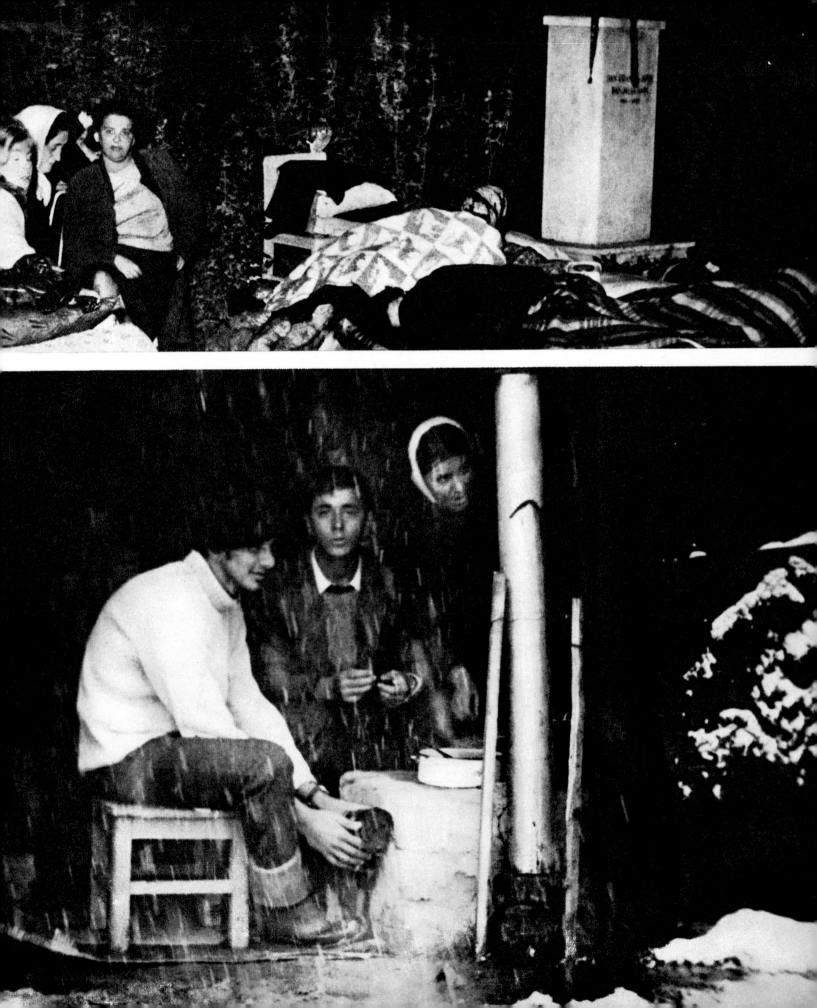

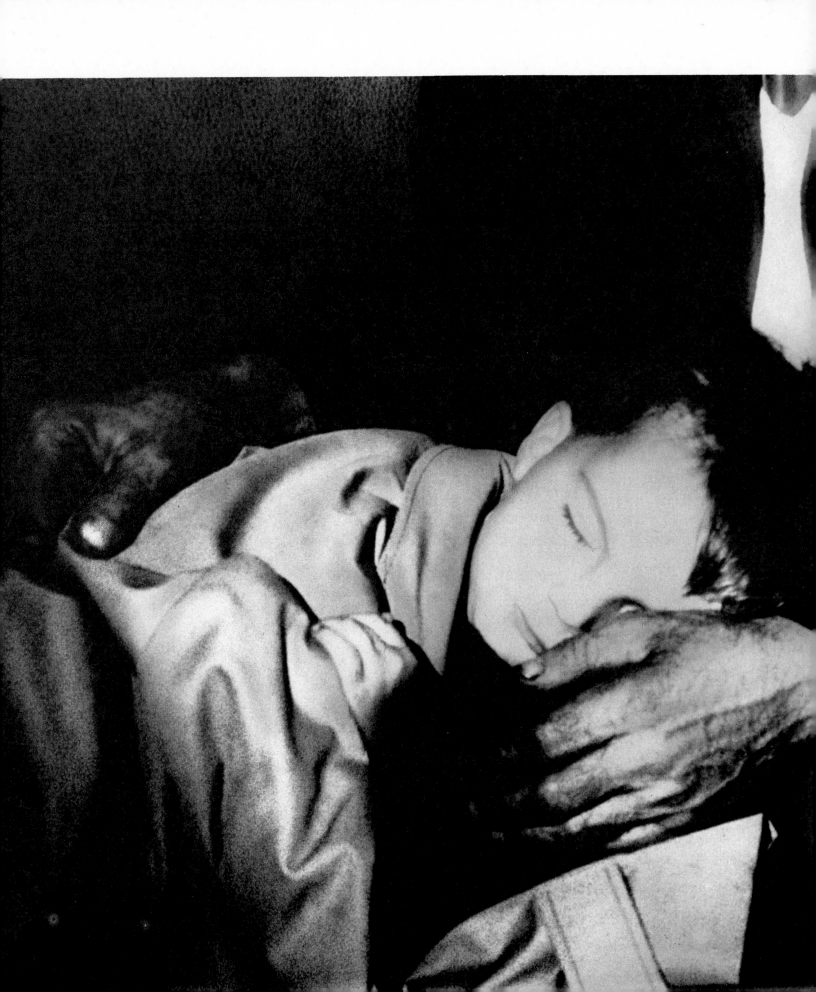

Provisional dwellings —
trailers and railway cars.

Alojz Ćurić,
Cracks and Saint George
— drawing

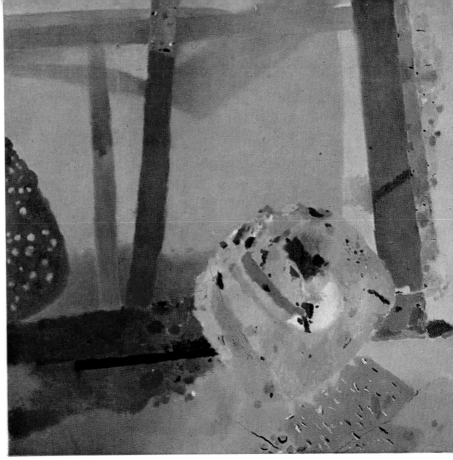

Dušan Simić (1930—1961), Self-portrait

Bekir Misirlić, Tombstone by the Window

Kemal Širbegović, Landscape

Mersad Berber, Interior

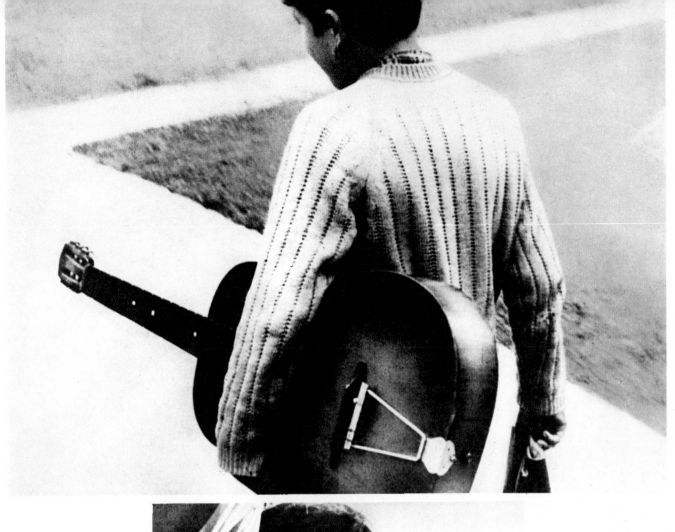

Your most important concern should be the people, every man, every child...
Tito

Damages caused by the earthquake, of a greater or minor extent, were recorded in fifteen communes of the Bosnian Krajina. These communes are: Banjaluka, Čelinac, Laktaši, Bosanska Gradiška, Prnjavor, Kotor-Varoš, Mrkonjić-Grad, Skender-Vakuf, Srbac, Jajce, Ključ, Prijedor, Sanski Most, Bosanska Dubica and Bosanski Novi. In areas of the highest earthquake intensity (Banjaluka, Čelinac, Laktaši) there were even casualties: 15 citizens lost their lives, while more than 1,250 persons suffered more or less severe injuries.

The earthquake damaged or destroyed 86,000 flats with almost 3.7 million square metres of living area, 566 schools, 133 medical care buildings, 152 public administration buildings, 146 cultural institutions and monuments. The economy of the entire area involved in the earthquake suffered great losses. The earthquake also caused substantial costs for the evacuation and provisional accommodation of the population, for the food and supplies during the first days after the earthquake, for the evacuation of school students and their accommodation in other Yugoslav towns, for demolitions and clearing up, treatment of injured persons, and erection of provisional quarters. The total amount of the damages caused by the earthquake, as determined by the Committee for Damage Evaluation of the Federal Executive Council, amounted — for all the affected communes of the Bosanska Krajina region — to 7 billion and 150 million dinars.

The town of Banjaluka and it closer environs suffered the greatest damage. The earthquake affected, to a large extent, and disabled the backbone of the town's economy, of its industry and mining, agriculture, forestry, building construction, transportation, trade and catering, crafts, communal utilities — altogether 112 enterprises. Among those hit the most were the Cellulose and Viscose Factory, the largest industrial plant in the Bosanska Krajina region, then the Vrbas Wood and Timber Industry (some plants of this enterprise were completely destroyed), the Vitaminka Fruit Juice and Canning Factory, the Budućnost Building Material Works, and the Glas Newspaper Enterprise whose facilities were completely destroyed. The buildings of the Trudbenik Ready-made Clothing Factory suffered the same fate. Considerable damage was also reported by other enterprises: the Jelšingrad Machine Works and Steel Foundry, the Rudi Čajavec Works, the Tobacco Factory, the Bosna Footwear Factory, and other industrial plants. The business facilities of Banjaluka's trading organizations were also considerably reduced owing to damage. Two of the greatest trading organizations, Krajinauzor and Metal, were deprived of one-half of their business space.

The earthquake also wrought particular damage upon utility plants: water supply system, sewage and traffic arteries. Along with the buildings, the enterprises also suffered substantial loss through damages of equipment and stocks.

The housing fund of Banjaluka was damaged to a terrifying extent. 36,276 flats, with 1,632,968 square metres of area, were damaged or destroyed. Medical facilities and equipment were completely wrecked: 61 buildings with 45,269 sq. m. of useful area, and 28 welfare institution buildings with 14,622 square metres of area. In the commune of Banjaluka, the earthquake damaged and destroyed 131 school buildings with 82,503 square metres of area.

The cultural institutions and monuments were also heavily struck by the earthquake. Among the severely damaged or destroyed buildings we find Ferhad-Pasha's Mosque, the Watch-tower, the Arnaudija Mosque, the trappist church and monastery in Delibašino Selo, the Culture Hall with the Art Gallery, the Museum of the Bosanska Krajina, the church in Krupa on the Vrbas, Sofi Mohammed-Pasha's Mosque, the Gomionica monastery, and the old burg — the Kastel. 38 public administration buildings were also damaged or destroyed, with 27,191 sq. m. of useful area, and additional 35,244 sq. m. of area in other buildings beloging to the socialist sector.

The commune of Laktaši also suffered major ravage. The earthquake damaged and or destroyed 6,267 houses, 44 schools and cultural institutions, 13 medical care buildings, and 2 public administration buildings. The Prnjavor commune also suffered heavily, especially the Tannery and Footwear Works; besides, the earthquake damaged or destroyed 8,841 houses, 38 schools, 37 cultural buildings, 10 health institutions, and 13 administrative buildings. In the commune of Čelinac, 3707 houses, 20 school buildings, 5 cultural buildings, 2 health and 1 welfare institution, and 4 administrative buildings were destroyed and damaged. The Skender-Vakuf commune was also heavily affected by the earthquake, which wrecked 1,436 houses, 17 schools, and one cultural institution. The elements did not spare most of the Bosanska Gradiška commune either; the most important enterprises in the commune were heavily damaged, i. e. the Radnik Timber and Furniture Factory, and the Mladen Stojanović Farm and Food Processing Plant. In the villages at the foot of the Kozara mountain, the earthquake wrecked 9,572 houses, 45 schools and 16 buildings of a cultural character, 5 medical buildings and 14 administrative buildings. Although the earthquake was not felt — in all its intensity — on the entire territory of the Jajce commune, the material damage was very high: 899 houses, 19 schools, 1 cultural building, 6 medical and 8 administrative buildings. In the very town of Jajce, the earthquake damaged important monuments from the period of the Bosnian-Herzegovinian state, and monuments from the recent history of the peoples of Yugoslavia: the Jajce Fort with the gates, the Bear-Tower, the Esme--Sultan Mosque, the Watchtower, the Museum of the Antifascist Council of the People's Liberation of Yugoslavia, and the Memorial Building of the Regional Antifascist Council of the People's Liberation of Bosnia and Herzegovina. Most of the Bosanska Dubica commune also felt the destructive force of the earthquake: 1,063 flats, 28 schools, 5 cultural institutions, 7 health and 13 administrative buildings were either destroyed or damaged. The old monastery of Moštanica also suffered serious damage. The communes of Bosanski Novi, Prijedor, and Sanski Most were affected by the earthquake only in some parts, but its action — in the areas involved — caused serious material damage. In the Bosanski Novi commune, 568 flats, 37 school buildings, 6 cultural institutions, 4 health and 6 administrative buildings were damaged or destroyed. The Dervish--Tower in Blagaj was also considerably damaged. In the Prijedor commune, the earthquake wrecked 4,903 flats, 41 schools, 13 cultural institution buildings, 11 health and 10 administrative buildings. Among the historical monuments, the old burg Kozarac suffered the greatest damage. In the anski Most commune, the figures are: 809 flats, 40 schools, 3 cultural institution buildings, 3 health and 9 administrative buildings. The old town of Kamengrad, and the prayer square in Kamengrad, were also heavily damaged.

Major material damage was caused by the earthquake in the communes of Ključ and Mrkonjić-Grad. In the former, 2,470 flats, 36 schools, 4 cultural institution buildings, 3 health and 7 administrative buildings were either destroyed or damaged. Substantial damage was also suffered by the mediaeval town and fortress of Ključ, in which the last Bosnian king — Stjepan Tomašević — was killed in 1563. The Mrkonjić-Grad commune suffered the following loss: 3,174 flats, 32 schools, 6 cultural institution buildings, 3 health and 13 administrative buildings. The following important historical monuments were also damaged: Kizlar-Aga's Mosque (one of the oldest in Bosnia and Herzegovina), and the Memorial Museum of the Regional Antifascist Council of the People's Liberation of Bosnia and Herzegovina. The Kotor-Varoš commune was also affected by the earthquake: 1,372 flats, 22 schools, 1 cultural institution building, 1 health and 7 administrative buildings were destroyed or damaged. In the Srbac commune, the outcome of the earthquake was the following: 4,630 flats, 24 schools, 14 cultural institutions, 3 health and 5 administrative buildings.

MAP OF EPICENTRES AND MACROSEISMIC INTENSITY OF $I_0 \geq V°$ MCS EARTHQUAKES IN NORTH BOSNIA

FOR THE 1901 - 1969 PERIOD

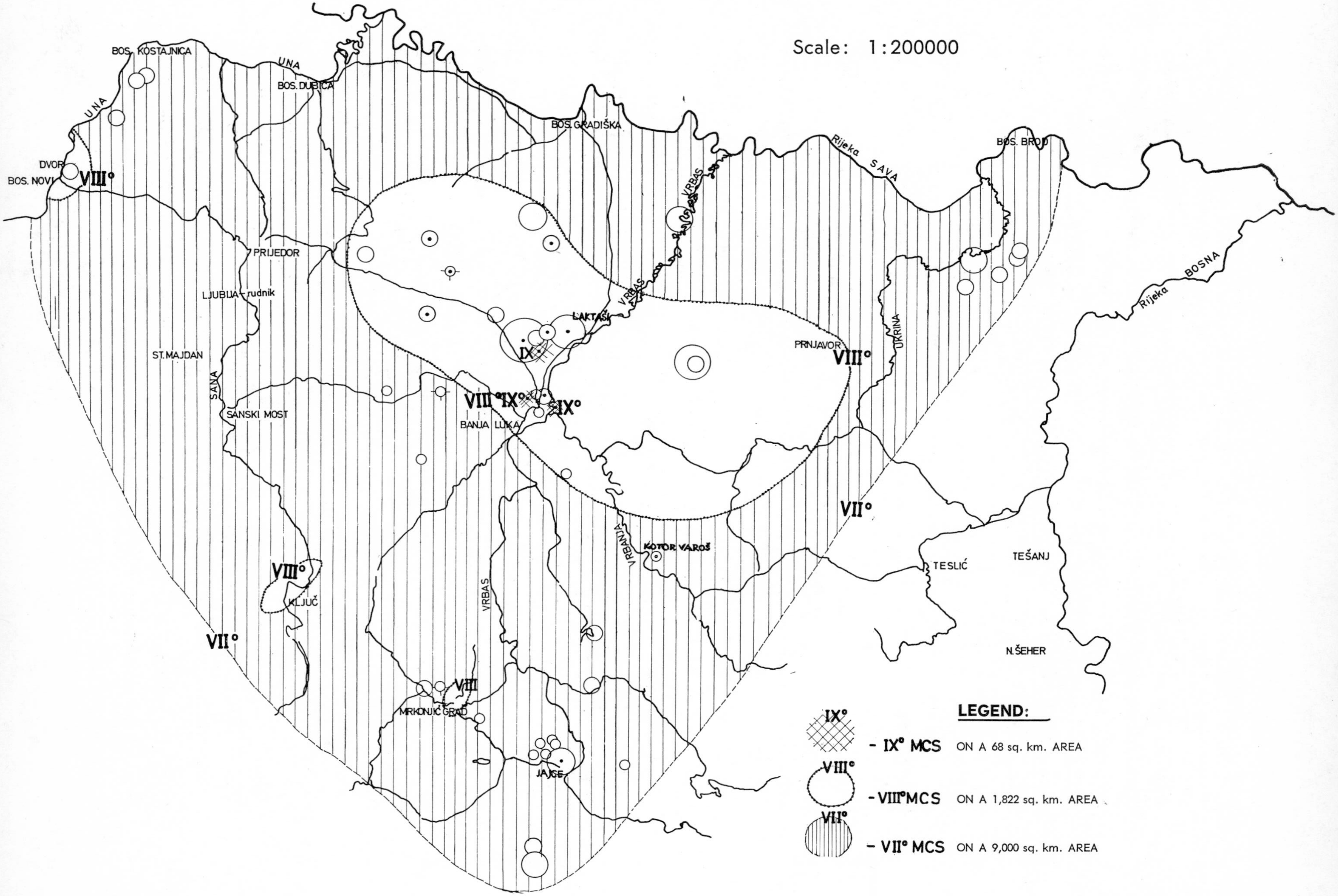

Scale: 1:200000

LEGEND:

IX° — IX° MCS   ON A 68 sq. km. AREA

VIII° — VIII°MCS   ON A 1,822 sq. km. AREA

VII° — VII° MCS   ON A 9,000 sq. km. AREA

The seismic activity in the Krajina region (bordered in the north by the river Sava, in the west by the river Una to Bosanski Novi, in the southwest by the Bosanski Novi—Jajce line, and in the east and southeast by the Jajce, Teslić and Derventa areas) may be followed — on the basis of data published in Yugoslav and other seismological publications, and of macroseismic ground surveys — over a longer period of time: from the middle of the 19th century to the present day.

According to incomplete data, the strongest earthquake in the Bosanska Krajina region (7 degrees according to the Mercalli scale) was recorded in 1861, with the epicentre between Bosanska Kostajnica and Bosanska Dubica. Later on, weaker earthquakes were periodically felt near Banjaluka (1866), as well as somewhat stronger ones (1885). No data were recorded regarding the epicentres. On May 20, 1888, a "violent earthquake" (according to the written record of the event) alarmed the inhabitants of Banjaluka. After a period of "peace", the earth shook again near Banjaluka on February 26, 1891. A series of earthquakes, with a gradual increase in intensity, ended in a stronger quake on March 27, 1897. Weaker ground tremors were also felt in 1899.

Earthquakes of varying intensity were felt alternatively, in different intervals, in the Banjaluka and Jajce block from 1901 to 1968. Seismic activity of lower intensity was recorded, from time to time, in the 1901—1907 period in both areas. Twenty-odd months of no activity followed, and then — again — a series of earthquakes (with greater or shorter intervals) over a period of eight years. From 1917 to 1935 several weaker earthquakes were felt in the Banjaluka and Jajce area, as well as periods of seismic inactivity. A series of earthquakes, of a varying intensity, was felt in Banjaluka from the 3rd to the 29th October, 1935. There were altogether 11 earthquakes. The strongest ones, of the 7 degree order, were felt on October 11 and 21. On that occasion minor damage was recorded in Budžak and some other villages in Banjaluka's environs.

No stronger earthquakes appeared in this region up to 1950. In the latter year, on August 31, an 8 degree (Mercalli scale) earthquake shook Dragovići, Hrvaćani and other near-by villages. Most of the damage was felt in the village of Dragovići, where ten or so houses were destroyed or damaged.

Before the appearance of disastrous earthquakes in the Bosanska Krajina region in October 1969, earthquakes of a lower intensity were recorded in the environments of Banjaluka: 1966 — near Bronzani Majdan (4 degrees Mercalli), 1967 — west of Čelinac (5 degrees), 1968 — north of Laktaši (5 to 6 degrees). On September 16, 1969, a weaker 4 degree earthquake was felt west of Kulaši.

The series of strong earthquakes started on October 26, 1969. Two of these were disastrous: the 7.5 degree earthquake on October 26, and the 8.5 degree one on October 27. The horizontal and vertical movement of the ground caused major wrecking and damage in Banjaluka and sixteen neighbouring communes. A somewhat weaker impact, 6.5 degrees, again shook a great part of the Bosanska Krajina region on December 31, 1969. After the first October earthquake a series of ten weaker tremors followed. The same phenomenon occurred after the strongest earthquake on October 27, 1969. These additional earthquakes of a lower intensity are till taking place. The epicentre of the first earthquake was seventeen kilometres north of Banjaluka, that of the second twelve kilometres, also north of the town. Altogether 1,413 earthquakes were recorded during 1969. It is being considered that the total number is even greater since no instrumental readings of ground tremors were taken during the first eight days. Minor ground movements are still under way. Huge masses have been involved and the process of stabilization is obviously slow. Such a discharge of accumulated energy has also decreased the strength and the number of destructive earthquakes.

74 epicentres, ranging from 5 to 9 degrees of the Mercalli scale, were recorded in the Banjaluka region between 1901 and 1969. Five degree earthquakes were the most frequent. The maximum seismic intensity of 9 degrees referred to the shock of October 27, 1969. By the nature of their origin, all the earthquakes in this area are tectonic ones. They have appeared mostly at the depth of 15 to 20 kilometres. Outside the central — eight degree — zone round Banjaluka, Laktaši, Čelinac, Prijedor, Bosanska Gradiška and Prnjavor, minor zones of the same intensity are located round Mrkonjić-Grad, Ključ and Bosanski Novi. The general direction of the central zone is northwest — southeast. The form of the 7 degree isoseismic during the past tremors in this area is similar to the form of the 8 degree isoseismic during the October 1969 earthquakes. During the October 27, 1969, earthquake some parts of the Banjaluka zone — Vrbanja, Petrićevac and Trn — were under the impact of a 9 degree earthquake shock.

ARTICLES BY:

Mato Džaja
Milan Ferković
Zlatko Hadžiabdić
Ibro Ibrišagić
Miloš Janković
Boris Kandić
Besim Karabegović
Đuro Kečan
Zdravko Kukrika
Predrag Lazarević
Dušan Lukač
Drago Mažar
Branko Milanović
Limun Papić
Svetozar Pucar
Velimir Stojnić (People's Liberation War)
Miljko Šindić

PHOTOGRAPHS BY:

Kasim Alijagić
Vojislav Andonović
Nemanja Bojičić
Vladimir Dobričić
Ismet Ibrišagić
Uroš Hinčić
Pero Jakić
Slobodan Janković
Jovan Koledin
Mitja Koman
Mujo Kušmić
Stipo Martinović
Drago Mažar
Duško Momčilović
Aleksandar Ravlić
Milorad Škrbić
Miodrag Šobot
Zdravko Velimirović
Joco Žnidaršić

We have also used photographs from: the Bosanska Krajina Archives, the Bosanska Krajina Museum, the Museum of the People's Revolution in Sarajevo, the Secretariat for Information and Documentation of the Banjaluka Town Council, and the Regional Museum.

THE MATERIAL HAS BEEN COLLECTED, AND THE PHOTOGRAPHS SELECTED, BY:

Bekir Misirlić
Miljko Šindić
Enver Štaljo

EDITORS:

Dr. Branko Milanović
Miljko Šindić, M. S.

COLLABORATORS:

Živko Babić, Savka Basta, Ismet Bekrić, Jovan Bojović, Ranko Ćurčija, Alojz Ćurić, Mak Dizdar, Irfan Horozović, Josip Jović, Niko Jurinčić, Momir Kapor, Osman Karabegović, Drago Kolak, Dušanka Kovačević, Custodians of the Regional Museum and of the Bosanska Krajina Museum, Tihomir Lešić, Dušan Lukač, Šefket Maglajlić, Faik Mehanović, Ranko Pavlović, Draško Popović, Milorad Popović, Milan Šipka

TRANSLATED BY:

Janko Paravić

READER:

Milan Šipka

PRINTED BY:

Grafički zavod Hrvatske, Frankopanska 26, Zagreb, 1970